Beauty & Chaos

The Inside Story of a Recovered Addict

CHRISTOPHER RIZZO

Fulton Books
Meadville, PA

Published by Fulton Books 2022

ISBN 979-8-88505-819-3 (paperback)
ISBN 979-8-88505-820-9 (digital)

Printed in the United States of America

CONTENTS

PREFACE

The intention of this book is to inspire anyone and everyone looking for a deeper understanding of life. The best way I know how to pass on the message to the next suffering man or woman is by going into detail of the way my life used to be, how it is now, and my perspective of the future. Everything we say and do is a reflection of how we see ourselves and how we see the world—consciously and unconsciously. Every day, every minute, we have a choice on how to respond to our environment and what life throws at us. We are painting and creating the picture of our future with every action we take. The paintbrush is always in your hand.

I'm not writing because I think I'm a good writer. I'm writing to document important and valuable information. I believe there are a lot of people in the world that are like me in that they are craving spiritual wisdom. I'm not trying to convince anyone that I'm spiritually wise; I believe I'm only scratching the surface of what is possible. But I know I'm on to something good. This is the type of good that should be shared with anyone who is seeking it. I wouldn't be doing the universe any favors by keeping this information all to myself. To put what I have learned on record, I must tell my story of past, present, and future.

When I started writing this book, I wasn't sure if I would live long enough to finish it. My drug addiction was so unmanageably bad I truly believed that I was doomed to fail. I had so many secrets, hidden thoughts, and feelings that I felt it was very important for me to document my life in such a way that it would help explain some things that I have kept in the dark to my family, to shed some light as to who I was as a person. This was because I truly felt like I was running out of time, and I didn't know what else to do but to write somewhat of a love letter / goodbye letter to my friends and family. Then, as my sobriety became stronger, I decided to leave everything as it was but add lessons that I have learned along the way. Now, much of this book has become mostly what I've learned before and during my sobriety.

Thank you to all those who doubted me. Part of that was my fuel to succeed. Thank you to all those who believed in me. It was you who picked me up when I fell. Now I stand tall and defy gravity every day.

Chapter 1

In the Beginning

I can still remember a time when I would wake up happy and ready for life, ready to take on the day. *Bring it on, world! I got this! I can't wait to see my friends. Maybe today is the day I finally get the courage to ask out that pretty girl who crosses my path at least once a day.* She danced around in my imagination constantly. I had so much ambition. I had so many dreams—dreams I was sure I would live. This enthusiasm was way before any of the terrible things that were about to happen a couple years down the road. But I didn't know. I was still under the spell of being young and naive. Looking back, I realize that I am truly lucky to be alive. I am lucky to be where I am right now. I am lucky to still have my health and sanity.

Going to sleep and waking up are very difficult for me. When I'm up, I can't wait to go back to sleep. And when I wake up, I get mad because I'm not dreaming anymore. Then pain sets in. Memories come back. My responsibilities start screaming in my face. Then I start wishing I was somewhere else or, at least, dreaming again.

What is your earliest memory? I have an image of my preschool teacher holding me under my arms, dunking my feet in paint, then placing my feet on a piece of paper. I have an image of me sitting at my desk, struggling to write my name in script. I have images of playing outside of my parents' apartment: playing with toys in the mud, playing with toys on the staircase. There are images of my mom at the kitchen sink with me dancing to sound of the dishwasher. Images of me sitting under the dining room table, trying to match the tune of the vacuum with a long hum. I remember crying at the thought of myself dying at this early age. We were in the car coming home from somewhere, and I remember my mom asking me why I was crying. I don't think I had the ability to fully express what my mind was producing, but I think I said, "I'm afraid to die." That must have scared the shit out of them, huh?

According to psychology, this is a very important developmental stage. I'm guessing my earliest memory is from when I was about four or five years old. My personality was starting to develop. I was learning how to communicate. I was starting to form opinions of what I liked and what I didn't like. I was learning how to express myself. I can see that now, but I didn't see it then. You cannot explain the big picture theory to a five-year-old. So at five years old, where was I? Who was I? What was I supposed to do?

I was completely reliant on adults to take care of me. I got some freedom to do what I wanted for a little while, but for the most part, I was under the rule of whoever was watching over me. What does this teach a five-year-old? I'm sure it depends on the child and the environment. I believe we are all unique, and at the same time, we are all the same. The farther away you observe, all human beings start to look the same. The closer you get to the details, the more unique we get. With my situation, I started to learn that when I cried for something, I usually got it. When I would become very happy, loud, and energetic, I was told to quiet down. So maybe that's why I liked my room so much. I could play with my toys and let my imagination take the wheel. And no one could tell me to change or do something else. (I am starting to realize that writing this is a form of therapy for me. This is my way of releasing ancient memories, thoughts, and emotions.)

What was I crying for? I was crying for food. For attention. For the toy I just saw the commercial for. To go play with my friends down the block. That's pretty much what I still do today. What happened when I was told "Quiet down, stop that, go to your room"? I was being taught that being happy in front of people was wrong. I was not allowed to fully enjoy myself, my own existence, in front of authority. That has seemed to carry through as well. I have to maintain a certain composure at work. I have to maintain an acceptable composure in front of family and a nonthreatening composure in public. The only time I seem to be able to fully experience life and my existence is when I'm by myself. And am I really ever alone? If I play the music too loud, it disturbs my girlfriend. If I sing too loud, the neighbors will complain. I've gotten kicked out of bars and clubs for having too much fun.

I was born in 1983 and lived in Brentwood, Long Island, for the first ten years of my life. Brentwood in the eighties and early nineties was equal parts black, Spanish, and white. I never heard the word *minority* until much later in life when it was forced upon me. I made friends with people who I got along with. And I got along with just about everyone. It's not realistic to be friends with everyone. Some people are just schmucks. To this day, I still keep in touch with the friends I've made in Brentwood. I think that's amazing. I'm so happy we're still friends. I try to tell them that subtly sometimes without sounding too corny. I knew then that their skin color was different from mine, but that was never a problem. They were raised a little different from me, but that was never a problem. They ate different food from me, but that was never a problem. The only problem was we couldn't hang out as much as we wanted because there were such things as school nights and bedtimes and "My mom can't drive me today." Those were our major obstacles. That's it!

What was your first traumatic experience? My cousin Corey and I became close when we were growing up because our moms took turns watching us. We quickly became friends. Then we constantly made plans to see each other. He was older than me, so of course, I believed everything he said. I usually came to him with questions I had that I was too shy to ask my parents about. I think I was in third or fourth grade when one of the kids I went to school with told me that he saw his mom putting presents under the tree late on Christmas Eve night. I don't remember the entire conversation, but I remember being in class at that moment when I first felt the hollow feeling of doubt. The next time I saw Cousin Corey, I had to bring this up to him. I needed a second opinion. When I asked, his response was something along the lines of "I thought you knew…"

Now I know I was disturbed at this point. I lived the next year in complete denial of this haunting possibility. But I had to ask one more trustworthy source. I remember going to my parents' room. They were both there. I asked my mom, "Is Santa Claus real?" I remember a sad look in her eyes. She knew she was about to disappoint me. She didn't say anything, just shook her head from left to right. I was having a really difficult time with this. "What about the Easter Bunny?"

She said something like "No, sweetie."

Surely all the magic in the world couldn't disappear in one single night... "How about the Tooth Fairy?" She gave me one more slow shake of her head from left to right. I had no more questions. With my head down in confusion, I dragged my feet back to my room. I honestly don't know what was going through my mind at this point. But I know I was silent, still and drowning in confusion.

CHAPTER 2

ANALYZING MY CHILDHOOD DEVELOPMENT

My next traumatic experience was being forced to move to a new home with my family. At the time, I was one of two with a third sibling on the way. We moved farther east to a bigger house and a new school district. Soon after my brother was born, I had another sister. Now I was in a strange house, going to school with strange children, and I was the oldest of four siblings. And it was my responsibility to set the example.

It would be a long time until I truly understood compassion. The closest translation I received growing up was "Treat others like you want to be treated." Although I agree with this teaching, it was never really elaborated on. There is a hell of a lot more that goes into this way of understanding how the world works. As a young kid in my early teens, I was mainly concerned with fitting in with the cool kids. Do you think I could preach the teachings of compassion to the "cool kids" in my environment? Could anyone? Let me try it now…

Cherishing others is the supreme protection from suffering and enables us to remain calm and peaceful within. The ignorant mind of self-cherishing and self-grasping is the root of all suffering. Give up self-concern and work for the benefit of others. By cherishing others, we continually accumulate merit, and merit is the main cause of success in all our activities. We become a source of happiness and inspiration for everyone we meet. The wish to protect all living things from fear and suffering is the main cause of great compassion. We must reduce our obsessive self-concern. We need to keep a constant watch over our mind and learn to distinguish between the beneficial and harmful thoughts that are arising moment by moment. Those who are able to do this are truly wise.

Are you still with me? Did your mind start to wander as soon as it was asked to protect something other than itself? I know mine does. Our body and mind are connected and are an amazing piece of universal technology, but its main concern seems to be survival. How do kids "survive" junior high school into high school? By wearing the latest fashions, owning the newest trends, belonging to which ever clique they choose to try out for, agreeing with the beliefs of the collective group they want to be a part of, behaving in the accepted way of that group, and so on. I know this sounds familiar to just about everyone. And this behavior and mindset carries through all the way through adulthood. We conform to a society. We adopt and adapt. And then we become another brick in the wall. Another leaf on the tree. Another drop of water in the ocean. Individuality is not encouraged at this time. Although I wish it was. Sex suddenly becomes very important. And this is where the peacocks come out and display their feathers. Both male and female.

There I was, the new kid no one knew. I was in unfamiliar territory. But I could clearly see the dividing lines between the different groups forming. And of course, I started developing my first crush on a pretty girl in my class. Even though she sat next to me, she was a million miles away. What do I do? The only one really talking to me was the teacher. But she was not trying to be my friend. I remember starting to make friends when the teacher split us into groups to work on whatever project was assigned that day. This was when my shyness kicked in.

I didn't want to be the first to speak. I don't know why. Maybe because I was the new kid and I felt like I was intruding on their territory. I was the alien. I was the outcast. I definitely did not feel accepted in any way yet. But this was a fight-or-flight moment. Instead of fighting for my right to exist in that classroom, in that school, I cringed and I shrank. I was running away instead of standing my ground. Metaphorically. I was there, but I was afraid to participate. I was afraid of the judgment I might face if I said the wrong thing, if I did the wrong thing. I was frozen inside with fear.

I remember anytime I was ever called on to speak in class, my face would turn bright red with embarrassment. And some of the kids called me out on it, which made it worse. I had trouble reading out loud in class because of this terrible shame I couldn't understand. I would stutter and stumble over the words. The teacher thought I had a reading disorder and almost put me in the special education class. I never really spoke much unless someone asked me something. I was becoming known as the quiet kid. Oh how I hated being known as the quiet kid. The kids I became friendly with were the ones that were behaving similar to me. But they had their own reasons for being geeks. I don't think there is anything wrong with being a geek or a nerd, but that's just what we were called.

This is my attempt to find out what the fuck went wrong. Why am I the way I am right now? How did I get like this? Why do I sometimes wish for the sweet release of death? When did I give up? Why? When did I start to allow myself to deteriorate instead of grow? Why was I filled with hate? Why did I reject love? Why did I rebel? Why can't I shake the evil thoughts? Why can't I be content with what I have? Why do I like destruction? Why can't I be comfortable within my own existence? Why don't I have more patience? If I know what the right thing is, why do I do the wrong thing? Why can't I be content within my own existence? Why must I always wish and strive for more, more, more?

CHAPTER 3

AN EARLY INTRODUCTION TO CHAOS

We have pictures of me as an infant in my grandpa's lap as he is feeding me from his beer bottle. Was that the moment I became an addict? I remember riding around in my dad's pickup truck as a young kid, and he would teach me how to hold and sip from a beer bottle correctly. Was that the moment I became an addict? I remember my cousin asking me to try what the Indians called "fire water." It was his dad's whiskey. Was that the moment? Probably none of those times. I don't regret any of those moments. I love them and the people that were there. How about in eighth grade when I would not tell the complete truth about where I was going? When I would go into the woods near our house and start small fires. Or when we broke empty beer bottles in the street for fun. Or when we would go to the nearest store that sold trading cards and stole them, pockets full. Then we stole clothes. Then we stole lacrosse sticks. Then we got sloppy, and I got caught stealing sneakers. Instead of calling my parents when we got caught, I called my at-the-time girlfriend's dad, and we got reamed out by him. Better him than my dad, right? We threw water balloons at moving cars from the roof. We learned how to use a magnifying glass, manipulating the sun through the glass, and burned dead leaves until they caught on fire.

Why? Why all the rebelling against the rules? Why risk my freedom? Why was it so much fun? Was it part of being a kid? Why was I drawn to this behavior? Because not everyone I hung out with was into this kind of stuff. It doesn't matter where you go. Good and evil exist everywhere. To some, evil is more attractive, I guess. But why me? Why did I like it? Why do I still like it? Hang on. I know I like danger, but I'm not completely reckless. I like to think I took calculated risks. Not kamikaze missions. The probability of me getting away with these small crimes were high. And I think I knew that.

This looks like the age of me mastering the art of manipulation, testing the waters. I found out that drinking and smoking a little weed from time to time would not kill me, unlike what the commercials said that would threaten me about the dangers of drugs. In fact, once I started drinking and smoking with the cool kids, I became more and more accepted by the group. Why did I want to be accepted by the group? I wanted to be a part of something. I wanted friends. I wanted the pretty girls to notice me. I wanted to tell them what I thought, how I saw the world. I wanted them to adopt my ideas too. I wanted to listen to their music and wear their clothes. One day, I would own a car, too, and life would be perfect.

I took my road test, and by some miracle, I passed on my first try. By the end of the test, I was shaking so hard from the nervousness I had to lie down in the passenger seat while my dad drove all the way home. This was when I was given the privilege of driving on the road with the rest of the pedestrians. But I didn't see it as a privilege. I saw it as how it was finally my time to drive on my own, fly on my own.

By this time, I was equal parts good and mischievous. I was playing high school football, basketball, and lacrosse. So I was leaning more toward the jocks. I was a starter in lacrosse for a little while. Second string most of the time everywhere else. Then after one winning basketball game, one of the guys on my team started break-dancing in the center of the court. I had never seen this before, and I was instantly fascinated. I was laughing hard at what I was looking at but in total amazement.

I asked him, "What the hell was that?" He told me his older brothers taught him how to break-dance and still do. So of course I asked, "Would they teach me?"

He said, "I'll teach you. Come over this weekend, and we can practice at my house." From that moment on, I was a break-dancer. I was into sports all throughout my life, but I never obsessed over learning or getting better at something like this. We practiced together constantly. I went to his house. He went to my house. We studied the moves we saw on music videos. We recorded them on a VHS tape and watched it over and over and over in slow-motion. We tried the move right there in the living room, on the carpet, at the risk of knocking shit over in our parents' house. We didn't care. We both wanted to get really good at this. So good that we would be the ones in the music videos and break-dance competitions. We went out to the nightclubs and tried our moves out live in front of the crowd. Those events were called teen night then. I'm not sure if bars still allow this anymore.

Either way, if there was a nightclub that allowed sixteen-year-olds in, we were there. At that time, they were all over the island. We hit them all. There was an underground lifestyle dedicated to break-dancing, and we were a part of it. We had T-shirts made of our dance crew, "Super Freeze Crew." We started recruiting other guys that wanted to join. We started the recreational dance club at our high school so we could dance in the open areas after school without getting kicked out. To maintain anonymity, I won't provide last names. But our core group was Chris Mo, Chris Me, Mike M., George A. and Chris R. (me). We danced at pep rallies and talent shows. We put on one hell of a show at our high school's March Madness basketball tournament half-time show. Someone has that videotape, but we forget which one of us has it. But trust me, we killed it that day!

I dropped all sports I was involved with in my life up to that point. The only thing I tried next was gymnastics but only to get better at breakin'. I didn't even compete at the gymnastic meets. The only reason I joined the team was to learn how to backflip and get better at my flares and UFOs. By eleventh grade, this was my identity. A break-dancer. A B-boy. I had found something I was really good at and could be a part of a group that accepted me as one of its leaders. We created a new clique at school, and I was all about it. I knew some of the jocks would talk shit about us. I'm sure a lot of people talked shit about us because we were different and doing our own thing. The gossip and shit-talking bothered me. The dividing lines always bothered me, still do. But if I was going to be an outcast, I had to do it my way.

Now I was sixteen and raging with hormones. I was finally able to drive. I had experience with stealing and starting fires. I was beginning to understand the mental manipulation of others. And my obsessive qualities were starting to form as part of my psyche. I had some trauma dealing with being lied to, being uprooted from my home, and dealing with the feeling of abandonment. I was having dreams about becoming a professional dancer. I occasionally drank and smoked weed at parties. What could go wrong?

CHAPTER 4

HEARTBREAK

What did I value in high school? What was I really learning? I think I was learning the intricacy of politics more than anything else. I didn't see it then, but I see it now.

There was a group of kids that hung out in the street, at dead ends, and in the car. Through one of my B-boy buddies, I was introduced to a new way of hanging out. These kids just liked to drink their malt liquor, smoke weed, and listen to music. And of course, bullshit. That's pretty much it. I quickly learned that this was where the girls were. We were too young to do anything other than hang out outside because we were too young to get into bars at that time. We were far away from where our parents could see us. And this was where I met the first girl I obsessed over. She didn't have any special skills or talents. But she was beautiful. Lazy but beautiful. Me and my addictive personality had found a new target.

I really liked her. She had a carefree sense of humor and just a carefree vibe all around her. I was instantly intrigued by her and her lifestyle. I had to talk to her every day. I would have been with her every day if I could have. But we were both under our parents' rule at that age. I started spending more time with her than I was with my dancing. I was now a senior in high school, and I was forced to make college-based decisions. What would be my major? Where would I go to college? I looked into dancing as a career, but it just didn't seem realistic. I was considering starting a family on a dancer's salary. Did dancers even make a salary? I took a BOCES class in carpentry during my twelfth grade year, and we had a lot of fun in that class.

That carpentry instructor put the idea of becoming an architect in my head. So when it was time to apply of a college major, that's what I went for.

My first year of college was tough. I didn't really like making tiny models in class and having to explain my "theory" to the class. The professors seemed to hate everything I did. I did all right in my core classes. But I just really missed my girlfriend. She was one year behind me, so now I was seeing her a lot less. College started handing out a lot of homework, and I couldn't be with the one I loved. Sorry, I meant the one I was obsessing over. When I would call her to say hi, she would be out with other friends. Instant jealousy! I didn't care who they were, all I knew was she was with them and not me. This was when our relationship became me versus them.

Now I was dealing with a "me versus them" perspective. *They have what I want. You have what is mine.* Now a possessive quality took over me, and I told her, "I don't like the people you're hanging out with. I know you're all partying over there, and those guys are definitely attracted to you and hitting on you." I would make demands. "I don't want you hanging out with them anymore! Why can't you just wait for me?" Long spaces of us not seeing each other drove me crazy. For some reason, I was convinced she was cheating on me. At first, I questioned her innocently. Then my accusations became more aggressive. We were getting into fights over the phone constantly because of my jealousy. This had never happened before. We would hang up angry at each other. A short time after those angry hang ups, I would try calling her back to apologize or try to continue working it out. But she wouldn't answer my calls. That silence killed me the most. The ignored phone calls. The not-answering. That drove me to point of insanity when she wouldn't answer my phone calls. I called over and over and over. Which, to her, made me look even crazier. My frustration with her caused our fights to go on even longer. My jealousy and insecurities drove her away. I couldn't see this then, but I can see it clearly now.

We broke up during my second semester into college. I fell into a deep depression. I felt hollow inside. All the magic in the world and in me was gone. All of it. I stopped going to class. I stopped trying so hard to do well. The light and the life in me were dead. I had no idea who I was or where I was going. I have never been sadder in my entire life. My personality was gone. My individuality was gone. My identity was gone. I remember going to her mother's house to see her, but her mom stopped me in the driveway and wouldn't let me in. There was no way I could hold back those tears. I even pleaded with her mom for her to give me another chance. The only insightful thing I can remember her saying was "In time you will heal." My immediate question was "How much time?"

CHAPTER 5

MY EARLY TWENTIES

During this time, I got a job working construction with a small residential carpentry crew at sixteen years old. I was still interested in architecture and thought it was a good idea to get some field experience. We mostly worked on residential renovations in the suburbs of New York. I learned a lot with this crew. This was a good group of guys. It was a small company, so everyone knew everyone. We spent a lot of time together on those construction sites, and the old-timers would talk about women and reminisce their good old days. The experienced guys took me under their wing as an apprentice. Each one of them taught me their own specialized tricks of the trade. Then there were the junior mechanics who also took me under their wing as their helper, but I had an easier time relating to the younger guys simply because we were closer in age.

I came into the company a fanatic of hip-hop: the style, the music, the history, and the language. After a year of working with these guys, I was a rock-and-roll enthusiast. That's all they played on the radio. This was my school of rock. It took me a while, but eventually, I opened up to these guys. They were consoling and encouraging. They also broke my balls constantly for being the rookie with no experience. During my first couple of weeks with the company, they saw that I had no personality left because of my heartbreak, and they gave me shit for it. After a little while, when I got to know them a little better, I started giving that shit right back to them. The old-timers took us to bars and strip clubs after work and showed me how to "unwind."

The lead foreman really pushed me hard during work hours. He saw I was greener than green, but I also think he saw potential in me. I was physically fit and young, and I wasn't afraid to work hard. His famous words were "Do it like a man!" He would rip the hammer out of my hand, or whatever I was using, and say, "This is how a man does it!" I would pay close attention to his form. There was an art form to how he was moving. It's all physics, really. You have to incorporate balance, gravity, weight, wind, torque, and strength into what you were doing. All with a gentle yet firm grip and stance. When an experienced carpenter is working, it's like poetry in motion. It sounds funny, but this man's movements were engraved in his muscle memory from years of doing this kind of work. He knew his next five moves while still working on the first motion. He had his entire day planned in each movement he made. And after each advancement was made, he was mentally working on the next five steps needed to keep it moving. This was how these guys taught me to work.

It was a slow and steady pace, but we got a lot of shit done every day. Honestly, it reminded me of dancing. But after this dance was over, we were standing on top of a brand-new house. I never got too friendly with Dennis because he was always such an asshole to me. But I love him for it because he turned me into a carpenter really quick. The annoying but great thing about being a carpenter is that you can always get better at mastering your trade. There is always someone trying to come up with an easier, faster way to get the same thing done. There are new tools and technology constantly being upgraded to make our workday easier. And also, the building codes keep upgrading. And better, stronger material is always being made. After a while, I was coming up with my own tricks. This was all fun when I was young and new to the construction game. I wasn't really feeling any pain, other than a little soreness. But it wasn't anything that was preventing me from getting up out of bed.

The boss must have seen some nice profits that year because he hired a new mechanic. He had about seven years on me. He was good. And I was jealous because I knew he was making more money than me. It wasn't long before we became friends. He had something to offer that I still knew very little of. He had been spending many years in the underground house-music clubs in the city. To me, this was the big-time, really cool stuff. This was mainly because I wasn't twenty-one yet and couldn't get into those clubs. But he would tell me all about it. Oh my god, I hung on to his every word. I went from hip-hop to rock and now to house music. Craig introduced me to cocaine, ecstasy, and the dark, trippy world of trance house clubs.

Occasionally, he would invite me over to his apartment, which was about a five-minute drive from my parents' house. I would get there, and he was already shaving down and cutting the coke into as fine a powder as he possibly could while listening to house music with porn on the muted TV screen. *Playboy* magazines were spread out across the glass coffee table in the middle of the living room. His wife was there too. She got down just as much as him. This was before they had kids. They had been married for a few years, and I guess they were waiting a little while before they started a family.

The sixty bucks I threw down lasted all night, and this was really good stuff. This was my first time doing a lot of drugs in one sitting, so I was opening up new synapses and passages in my brain that had never been there before. These were the years when drugs were fun. I wasn't helplessly addicted yet and didn't really start to get cravings yet. It was new and exciting. I was young and felt no pain, naturally. It would be a long time before I started using the words *hungover*. When I woke up after drinking and drugging all night, I was pretty much still drunk or high. And I liked it. I don't remember it being painful until much later.

At this point, I was twenty-one years old. I had dropped out of college, and I was working a steady construction job during the day. I would go home after work, eat dinner with my family, shower, and then go out partying all night. I wasn't going to the nightclubs to break-dance anymore. We were going to bars, not dance clubs, so we could get wrecked. And I was hanging out with a completely different group of friends. All we wanted to do was get drunk and high and try to pick up chicks. This was my routine for the next couple of years. And once I hit twenty-one, the alcohol flowed in even faster. I completely gave up on school. I wasn't really thinking about my future. I was content with being a carpenter because I knew, the longer I stayed, the more money I would eventually make. I was still haunted by the painful memory of losing someone that I thought would be with me forever. I was frustrated with college because it didn't work out for me. And I wasn't willing to put in the necessary time and energy to do well in school.

It's difficult to remember my mindset and all the events during these years of my life. But it was when I was around twenty-two years old when I started drinking beer and smoking weed in the morning to feel "normal." I never wanted to feel completely sober. I never let myself come all the way down. All this drinking and drugging became expensive quickly.

I had a group of friends that I hung out with just about every day. George introduced me to Burt. Burt introduced me to Kelly. Kelly introduced me to Jenn. And on and on. We took turns driving around in our cars and smoking weed in parking lots and dead ends. One night, Burt and I had a genius idea. "We should sell weed!" We knew enough people to sell to, and we knew a couple local dealers. Brilliant! What could go wrong? I started off splitting half of an ounce with Burt. We made a couple phone calls to spread the news to as many people as possible. We went through everyone in our phone and told those people to tell their friends. It didn't take long until we became very busy. So busy that I quit my construction job and was getting by with selling weed to our friends. Then those friends told their friends, and within one year, I was driving all over Long Island selling weed from the moment I woke up to the moment I passed out.

During the day we were hanging out at someone's house, and at night, we always found some kind of gathering that we turned into a party. I remember being happy during this stage of my life. I was known to everyone we hung out with as the weed dealer and a generous one. I always had a blunt rolled to get things going. I was in constant contact with so many people. We were going to house parties every other night and bars and dance clubs on the weekends. I met so many women. We visited friends in college who were living in the dorms at that time. Philadelphia, New Jersey, Upstate New York. My favorite places to go were the New York City dance clubs. That music and environment was unmatched no matter where I went. Everything was going great. My life was one big celebration. Until I got arrested for the first time and charged with marijuana possession.

I didn't see it then, but I see clearly now. Burt and I were getting our weed through a local dealer, Alfredo. He lived in the lower part of Bellport. We did not have a problem going there to see him. But I'm pretty sure everyone else that lived there had a problem with us. We were the only white guys in sight. We were aware of this, but we didn't care. After all, Al was our longtime friend. We started off buying an ounce of weed off him. We didn't want to invest too much too soon. We really didn't know how fast we would blow up. And we were responsible with the money. We put our profits back in the "business," each time doubling the last amount we bought. An ounce to two ounces to a quarter pound to a half of a pound to a full pound of weed. We were buying a full pound of weed each time we went to see Al. We thought we were so cool. I mean, it's a pillowcase full of weed. It is breathtaking the first time you see that much. Anyway, we were selling a lot of weed to anyone that called us, even some of Al's customers. Us white boys didn't think this was a big deal. C'mon, we were buying pounds of weed from Al. We knew he was making money too. But us selling to his customers, that was an invisible line we should have never crossed. Because I think it was Al that set us up to get pinched.

We got a call from Al one night saying that he had a friend looking for a half pound. I didn't hesitate. I was all over it. Only thing in my mind was *Let's go make this money.* I was the driver and the supplier. Burt sat up front with me. Al was in the back with a girl I was seeing at time. I honestly forgot her name. But we weren't hanging out much more after the events of this night took place. So Al told us that his "buddy" would meet us in the Radisson Hotel parking lot right off Exit 63 of the Long Island Expressway. We were all there ready with the half pound in the back seat, and all we had to do was wait for the call that we were to go into the hotel and deliver the weed. While we waited, we rolled up a blunt and continued drinking our Colt 45s.

A couple minutes went by. Suddenly, there was a silver minivan that pulled up right in front of my car. Not in a parking spot. It was just blocking me from going forward. The side door opened, and two guys got out. They approached my crappy car very quickly. Shining their flashlights in my face, one of them tapped on the window and told me to get out of the car. They found the weed very quickly. They turned to each one of us individually and asked, "Whose is this?" No one said a word. He said, "No one wants to confess? All right, you're all going to jail!" To jail we went. I was pissed. Scared but also very mad. What the fuck! My life was going great until these assholes came and ruined it! They held us at the station as long as they could until we bailed ourselves out that same night. We all got hit with the same charge: possession of six ounces of weed. That's what it said on the ticket. Weird, right? Because I know that a half pound of weed is eight ounces. Where did the other two go? Corruption obviously exists.

This was the point that Burt no longer wanted to sell weed with me. He got scared and wanted out. I don't blame him. And I wasn't seeing that girl anymore. I found out her dad was a cop. I wanted to get as far from the police as possible. But Al and I continued to hang out and hustle together. I would still get my weed from him, but I became his driver and sometimes would take him to pick up some serious weight. Maybe it was the paranoia, but I was developing a suspicion that he wanted to take me out, to get rid of me somehow. Because getting arrested didn't do it. I was charged with a first-offense misdemeanor. It was a slap on the wrist and only made me mad. On the night that we got arrested and bailed ourselves out, I went back to get another half of a pound and made sure we made that sale. I wasn't going to let the cops win that night. I also took another vow that night. Now I was going to sell cocaine. Fuck it. If I was doing this, I was going all the way and not looking back.

Eventually, Al did get rid of me. He built up a trust with me by getting me to give him the money for my re-up of weed first. Then he would go get the weed on his own and bring it to me later in the day. He actually followed through with this a couple of times to gain my trust. But I hated it every time. I never trusted him completely. I never felt like I could. But I had no choice but to go through with this procedure because I didn't know anyone else that would sell a white boy a full pound of weed. One day I give him $1,600 for a pound of really good regs. That day, he never came back. Never answered my calls. I basically never heard from him again. I got burned. It hurt my money situation, but I still had enough to get some coke to keep my hustle alive.

Just like how I ran the weed business was how I ran the coke business. I bought an eight ball to get started. Then I was able to buy a quarter ounce, half of an ounce, until I got to buying a full ounce at a time. I was selling coke to a lot of the same people who I was selling weed to. Those friends told their friends, and in no time, I was up and running again—this time with cocaine as my main money-maker. I was still selling weed, but I was focused on the coke sales.

I noticed a pattern with the guys I was buying in bulk from. They were all black or Spanish. And even though they acted like they were my friends, I think they resented me. They did not like to see a white boy selling drugs and making money. I'm sure they saw it as me stepping on their toes. They did not want me to be successful. They all tried the same move that Al did to try to destroy me. They wanted me to give them the money first, and then they would give me the product later the same day or the following day. And they would always have this elaborate story about how they needed to collect money from all the little dealers so they could go to the big dealer with more money to get a better price. Kind of like Costco Wholesale. So this was my lesson learned when buying from dealers: "Never give the money first! Even exchanges only!"

Anyway, I was getting by in life just by selling drugs. I had no other income. I did this for years—just staying out late, partying, sleeping late, then waking up and drinking, smoking weed, and sniffing a few lines to get my day started. I would repeat this cycle every day. I apologize if this sounds glamorous because it wasn't. Sometimes I would get a job for a little while to keep my parents off my back. I know my dad was suspicious. He kept asking me, "Where are you getting money from?" I told him I had savings. But that was all bullshit, and I think he knew it.

This was when my life really started taking a steep decline. The difference from a weed-high environment to a cocaine-high environment is like day and night. With weed, everyone is happy and adventurous. With coke, everyone is hyper and paranoid, especially after the rush of the first hit is gone. The "good feeling" or cocaine high only lasts the first couple of minutes. After that you're just chasing that first high or trying to figure out the perfect balance of beer, liquor, and coke so you can stay up and party all night. Cocaine gave me some pleasure, but it mostly gave me pain. Since I was selling it, I always had access to as much coke as I wanted, anytime I wanted.

I was on coke just about every day for many years. During those times, everything in my life was on the decline. My circle of friends became smaller and smaller because no one wanted me around anymore. My longtime friends that knew me told me I was a different person when I was high. It was as if my soul was gone. My unique character was gone. I was a hollow shell of who I used to be. I was a bottomless pit of drugs and alcohol. Drugs had become my first priority. Everything else was secondary including my family, my friends, and my health. I was deteriorating from the inside out, and it was obvious to everyone except myself. I was trapped in this downward spiral. The only way I was making money was by selling drugs. My only "friends" were the ones I was selling to and getting high with. I was developing a serious addiction to drugs and alcohol. I couldn't keep a decent job because I showed up fucked up or hungover every day. And when I tried to stop selling drugs to take a break from the chaos, I couldn't because my phone just kept ringing. When that phone rings and there is someone on the other line offering good money, I had a hard time saying no. It was much easier to just go with it.

I was driving drunk basically everywhere I went. At night I was driving home high, usually paranoid that I would get pulled over and arrested for possession or a DUI. I found myself praying to God over and over to help me get home. Many nights it felt like my heart was going to explode, and I would pray to God to help me live to see another day. Almost every night I was praying to God, angels, saints, and past relatives to help me get home safe and to keep me alive. I prayed for protection. I begged the gods to keep me safe and unharmed. After a couple years of selling, I was praying to keep my freedom.

I was never very religious. But I always believed there is more to life than what we can see. I believed it then, and I still believe it now. I believe there are angels that watch over us and that we get some assistance from time to time. I also believe there are demons and evil forces acting upon us too. Somewhere along the way, we invite them in.

I knew I had to change something or I was sure to die. I needed a better way to make money, and a better way presented itself just in time at a local bar. I was invited to a dive bar in Patchogue to sell coke to a couple of drinking buddies of mine. It was a bar with an Irish name. Patty's or something. It doesn't matter. The guys I was selling to were all wearing the same sweatshirts that read "Licciardi Builders" on the back. I could tell it was a construction company, and I was looking for a real job. So I asked one of them what that was all about. They told me it was their family business, and they were looking for some help because the work was picking up. I took his number down and started work with the youngest of the brothers the following Monday.

This turned out to be a great opportunity for me. Through the Licciardis, I met their longtime friends who were musicians. These rock-and-roll guys took me in immediately. I couldn't figure out why, but they loved me. Townie, Murphy, Shatz, and Dan all wanted to know if I could sing. I shrugged my shoulders and said, "I'll give it a try." I spent the next four years working in the Hamptons framing houses during the day and playing in a rock-and-roll band at night. I was finally making good enough money where I could stop selling drugs to get by.

But I was still "experimenting." One of the guys I ended up working with a lot introduced me to Vicodin on one of my hungover days. Tom said, "Take two of these. It will make you feel better." It definitely did, but I passed out at lunchtime. I was hooked from then on. Whenever I wasn't feeling well; if I was a little tired, bored, or anxious; if I was about to go to some social event; if I had done too much coke; if I was uncomfortable in any way, I was taking opiates to feel "better." I guess that was the belief in my mind. I would hear "This will make you feel better" even if I was feeling okay. Who doesn't want to feel better?

And I didn't just feel better, I felt invincible, pain free. When I was high, everything was great. I didn't have a care in the world. I was spending all my money, but I didn't care. I was missing a lot more days of work, but I didn't care. I wasn't giving my relationships the energy they deserved, but I didn't care. I lost more friends because they were disgusted by me. I didn't care. I was pawning my jewelry for drug money, selling my work tools for drug money, selling my expensive clothing to thrift stores for basically pennies. I sold my music CDs back to Best Buy. I didn't care. As long as I had my heroin, everything was fine.

I transitioned pretty quickly from Vicodin to Percocet to OxyContin to heroin. My tolerance grew, and I needed more and more to get the same high. I needed stronger and stronger "medicine" to "feel better." I became addicted almost immediately, and with addiction comes the craving. I was able to stop selling drugs because I found a good job. But I couldn't stop doing the drugs because I had developed a lot of very bad habits over the years. And the worst habit of them all, I feel, is the belief that I need a substance to start my day. It started with smoking weed in the morning or drinking a little beer. Then it was taking Percocet in the morning to give me the "motivation" just to go to work. Soon after that I needed heroin in the morning just to gain enough "enthusiasm" to brush my teeth and take a shower.

I had two settings: high or not high. If I was high, I was talkative, a little obnoxious, and fun to be around. If I was not high, I was silent and angry. Angry to be alive. Angry I wasn't high. And I was definitely not fun to be around.

CHAPTER 6

THE DECISION TO GIVE COLLEGE ANOTHER TRY

It was 2008, and the economy had crashed because of a volatile real estate market that year. Sellers got greedier and greedier, and the buyers were buying homes they couldn't afford. Banks had to get bailed out by the government, and for some reason, the price of gas become more and more expensive. Then we reached a point where gas was almost impossible to find. We would drive around for miles looking for an open gas station. And if we found one, the line was ridiculously long. People were filling up their cars then their handheld gas cans. We all had to do it because we didn't know if this particular station would be open tomorrow. It was strange times.

More and more people became unemployed. Businesses went under. And since I missed one day per week at work, on average, I was one of the first to get fired from Licciardi Builders. Losing this job really hit me hard. That was how I made money. Money was how I maintained my shitty lifestyle. And without money, I couldn't pay the rent. I had to move out of that Patchogue house that I shared with two of my bandmates and moved back to my parents' house in Holbrook. I really had no other options. I really loved that Patchogue house though. The heating was terrible, my bedroom was small, but the basement was where our band practiced. To attend band practice, all I had to do was go downstairs into the basement of my own house. How cool was that?

Well, it wasn't cool anymore. We officially stopped playing when I had to leave that house. Playing with Clearview was some of the best years of my life. I'm not the greatest singer in the world, but I had a lot of fun. We only played original songs that I helped create, and I really felt like a rock star during those times. I was certainly playing the part. But our creativity as a band started to fade away because I couldn't stop getting high. I felt like a rock star, but I also felt like shit. The drugs and alcohol had a negative effect on my energy and creativity even though I thought it would enhance my energy and creativity. I had to get high before I did anything. I was drinking heavily and sniffing coke and shooting heroin often. Way too often. So much so that there wasn't any room for anything else in my life.

I moved back in with my parents. By this time, I was about twenty-five and addicted to very bad, very expensive drugs and unemployed. The first thing I had to do was find a job. The first thing I found was the first thing I took, which was working for a tree removal service. I lasted three weeks, at most. My job was to drag the tree branches to the chipper as they fell from the sky. The lead foreman was in the cherry picker with a chainsaw hacking huge branches off large trees and letting them fall to ground. That's where I was, waiting for these things to fall. Once they fell, I had to drag them to the chipper. Again and again and again. All day, every day. As the lead foreman got to trunk of the tree, the pieces got heavier and heavier. This truly felt like slave labor to me. There were no skills required. Just don't fall into the chipper.

I was probably complaining to my mom one day about this awful job when she said, "Why don't you go back to school?" I immediately rejected the idea. I had tried college and hated it. I was enrolled in the architecture program at NYIT for a year then dropped out. I was enrolled in business at Stony Brook for a year then dropped out. Then I tried psychology for a semester at Stony Brook then dropped out. I was enrolled in economics at Suffolk County Community College for a semester then dropped out. Are you seeing the pattern here? I was not interested in college at all in my early twenties because I was only concerned with getting drunk and high and hanging out with girls. Besides, I identified as a workingman. I learned the skilled trade of carpentry. I was able to build a house. But at this point, I was dragging tree branches to their death.

The next workday at lunchtime, I really started considering the idea of going back to college. *Maybe I should give college one more try. But what should I go for? I could try majoring in music…that would be fun, right? I could start a new band or try to make music on my own. Or maybe there's something I could do with construction…* I'd been working since I was sixteen. I felt like I had a lot of experience already, and I always admired the lead foreman on the job—the one who had the game plan in his head and gave the orders and directions to get the house built and the job done efficiently.

I brought up the idea to the people I felt the closest to: my godfather and my oldest friend from childhood, Frank from Brentwood. They both gave me the same answer but in different ways. My godfather said, "You don't need a degree to play rock and roll in a bar."

Frank said, "You're a hands-on guy. That's how you have always made your money—in construction. Go to a trade school."

It all made too much sense not to go for it. I was looking for something a little more professional than a completion certificate from a trade school, so I went online and looked up colleges offering construction classes. There were more than I thought there would be. Some colleges were too far or too expensive. But there was one college that was calling my name from the moment I saw the classes offered: Farmingdale State College of New York. They had a construction management bachelor program. Farmingdale was close to home, and I could pay for it through taking out student loans. Perfect! To make ends meet, I swallowed my pride and took a job waiting tables at night. My girlfriend at the time who used to bartend at TGI Friday's put a good word in for me, and I got the job. I wanted to be a bartender, too, but in the restaurant industry, they make you wait tables first because the food is the real moneymaker for the business. The drinks are just the extra cherry on top, as far as profits go. I still had a problem though. I was still addicted to heroin and cocaine. *Oh well,* I thought. *I'll make it work.*

To this day, I still do not know how I got through the next four years without completely failing out of college or dying from an overdose. Here was my routine: Class didn't start until around eight or nine a.m. This gave me enough time in the early morning to get my dope from a local dealer then get to class. I barely made it on time for each class. I usually shot up in my car a few blocks away from the school, lit up a cigarette, then drove into the school entrance with paper-thin confidence that I would blend in with everyone else. I was wearing a metaphorical mask that, I thought, looked like a young man pursuing his dreams of attending college.

The people I went to college with were mostly commuters just like me. From what I could tell, the attitude was get to class, take notes on the lesson, write down the homework assignment, then go back home to work on the homework assignment. There weren't many opportunities to make new friends. Or so it seemed. Because I had that same attitude, which was get in and get out then graduate.

But I was high as hell. I remember attempting to be the class clown. I commented on the professors' lessons, basically heckling them. Looking back, I'm so embarrassed of my behavior. I thought I was funny, but in reality, I was just being obnoxious. In between my wisecracks, I did pay attention and take good notes. I was attending extra help after class just about every day to do my homework because the math and physics is no joke in college. There was no way I could understand that shit on my own. Thank God the college had that extra help program, and thank God it was free. The tutors were students that were compensated for their time in the study hall.

I absolutely needed a secondary tutor, and I wasn't afraid to ask for help with my homework. If I had a big paper to write, I took it to the study hall for the tutors to look over what I had done so far, absorbed their critique, then completed the paper on the weekends. I was barely getting through my classes. Each night the homework took hours to complete. I was also waiting tables at night. Every day during the week I was exhausted and constantly hungover. After waiting tables at night, I was drinking mostly malt liquor because that's what I could afford, and I needed a way to unwind. Healthy habits were long gone from my lifestyle because I liked to shoot heroin to become carefree and completely accepting of my life and situation at that current time period.

Patience was never a character quality of mine. I was honored and grateful to be attending college, just like my grandfather instructed me to do. But I also resented the fact that I had to get through these next four years just to obtain a piece of paper that stated what I already knew I was, which was a qualified and competent person to be hired by one of the top general contractors in New York. Four years is not a long time in the grand scheme of things, but it's a long time to wait for something you really want.

So I got high to kill time. Then I drank because I liked the taste of beer and really enjoyed getting sloppy and slightly losing my equilibrium. Then I sniffed coke when I became too drunk to walk in a straight line and speak without slurring my words. The cocaine energized me enough to continue drinking without passing out where I stood. Then I would drink and shoot heroin again because too much cocaine causes nervousness and paranoia. I did this again and again until I ran out of money.

But I always made sure to save enough money for my morning routine, which was to shoot heroin to avoid withdrawal and get back to "normal." My only "friends" were the ones I was getting high with. Even though we saw each other every day, we were not true friends. We stole from each other and undercut the other whenever we had the chance. We stole and cheated our way through life to support our drug habits. This way of living taught me how to use people to get what I want, how to convince people to do what I wanted them to do. To maintain a heroin habit, the addict needs to learn the art of manipulation very quickly. Otherwise, the sickness of withdrawal starts to kick in, and the longer the addict experiences withdrawal, the more he would rather die.

During these four years of recklessness, I got a DUI, got arrested for needle possession, got my license taken away, and went on unemployment. These negative consequences didn't stop me. Even though my family insisted I take a break and go to rehab, I just kept going. I refused to stop going to school because I felt if I were to stop or take a break, I would never return. It was during my second year at Farmingdale that I was arrested for a DUI, got my license taken away, and was forced to go to an outpatient rehab program. It was a place for me to go to appease the courts and my family.

I had to get rides from my dad and my aunt Fran, who lived close by my parents' house. What a lifesaver she was! Because I knew if I didn't graduate and get that degree, I would be forced back into dragging tree branches to the chipper. Back to what I considered slave labor. It was the thought of taking steps backward that scared the shit out of me. This fear kept me showing up to class. But there were days that I had to go through withdrawal because the dealer wasn't around yet or because I was flat out broke and had nothing left to sell. Guys at school would tell me "You look so pale, are you okay?" I would mumble, "I'm fine," but we both knew I was not.

CHAPTER 7

FINALLY ACCEPTING REHAB

What was my plan for the future? To graduate college then get a good job so I could live independently. But how could I do that addicted to heroin and cocaine? At this point, I was really starting to doubt that I could keep this up forever. What the hell was I going to do?

My mom had been begging me to go to rehab for years. My only reason for not going was that I would have to stop going to college, and I just refused to take a break because of the fear of never returning and never getting the opportunity to finally graduate. The fear of not seeing my dream all the way through into making it a reality was my main reason for continuing this filthy habit, along with the fear of experiencing withdrawal and feeling physically uncomfortable to the point of suicide. My twisted perception saw my heroin use as a way to stay normal enough to keep going to class, completing the homework assignments, and passing the tests. But now I was approaching my senior year, and winter break was coming up. And at this point, rehab started looking really good.

My parents had kicked me out of their house because of my drug and alcohol abuse. They refused to enable me by providing a rent-free safe place for me to get high in. So I moved into a crappy little house that I had to share with three other strangers that were very similar to me. That living situation didn't even last one year. I was not able to afford the $500-rent cost. This was when Superstorm Sandy wiped out many of the Long Island homes that were close to the shore. Most of New York lost electrical power. This was when gasoline was hard to come by.

Winter was upon us, and I was dead broke. I was jobless again because I just couldn't keep up. I waited tables at Friday's, Outback Steakhouse, and a couple diners. I got hired and fired. Then I found a couple odd jobs here and there to keep me from completely drowning. The last job I worked before finally giving in to rehab was helping a crackhead install carpet in people's homes and offices. I know he was a crackhead because he would stop by my apartment all the time to smoke. I was his driver and the helper on the job. This guy underpaid me big-time. He would promise to pay me at the end of the week and usually shorted me money. Sometimes I wouldn't get paid at all. I gave up on him really quick.

Now I was out of a job with no money, no drugs, and no hope. I had made it through my third year of college, and now it was winter break. I was looking forward to my senior year of college, but I had enough of all the bullshit. I was so tired of lying, cheating, and stealing. I was tired of bargaining with pawnshops. I was tired of selling everything I had. I was tired of ruining relationships. I was tired of not being trusted. I was tired of never having enough gas in the car. I was tired of being so alone. I was tired of having everything getting taken away from me by my own actions. I was tired of always feeling hungry. I was tired of not having anything or anyone in my life. I was just tired.

I had to beg my dad to come and get me. I didn't have enough money or gas in my car to make it to him. This winter break was my chance to give rehab a try. Fuck it. I had nothing more to lose besides my life. I was terrified, but I went. It was also one of the conditions I had to agree to for being accepted back into my house again.

Chapter 8

Near-Death Experiences

Before I talk about the part when I start to clean my life up, I want to explore my many near-death experiences. I want to analyze what I had been doing with my life up until this point. What I want is for the reader to feel as if they are living through my real-life experiences, to see through my perception and to feel through my sensation.

I was told that while my mom was pregnant with me, my dad liked to poke her belly to feel me kick. With each poke, I would kick, turn a little more, and then turn a little more. When I was born, the umbilical cord was wrapped around my neck like a noose. The doctor said that I was lucky to be born alive. I have no memory of this, of course, but my imagination can't help itself from analyzing this situation. It was as if I was born into this world hanging from a noose. By some miracle, I escaped death the very moment I was brought into this world. Please do not misunderstand. I love my parents very much and do not blame them for any of my challenges, struggles, and close calls. The universe throws us curveballs and puts obstacles in our path. It is up to us to overcome them.

During the summer of fifth grade, I was almost hit by a speeding car on the highway. We liked to hang out in the woods just outside of the neighborhood, and we walked everywhere when we were kids because no one was driving yet, obviously. One day, my cousin Corey and I decided to cross the highway to get to the strip mall we liked to hang out at instead of taking the back roads that led to the wooded area that led to the parking lot behind the strip mall. It wasn't rush hour, but it was still a highway. We saw an opening, so we sprinted across to get to the dividing strip of land between the two opposite flows of traffic. We had one more three-lane distance to sprint across. I probably became a little overconfident and stopped paying attention to the cars coming toward us. I was right at the edge of the curb, about to step onto the first highway lane. But before I could get my foot down to the street, a car flashed by me. All I saw was the blur of a car speeding by me, no more than a few inches away from my face. The wind-force pushed me backward, and my heart skipped a few beats. I was frozen in shock. I was almost instantly killed. By some miracle, I hesitated a millisecond longer, and it saved my life. We were still stuck in the middle divider of traffic. We both felt it was better to keep going forward instead of going back. So before continuing, we waited for a mile-long break in between the cars so we could cross over the highway and onto the other side.

During my seventh-grade high school year, my appendix almost burst. Somehow, I was infected with appendicitis. My lower stomach region had been bothering me for a couple days, and the pain got worse every day. When I told my mom about the pain I was feeling, she convinced me it was gas. But this was an internal pain I had never felt before. It felt like I had swallowed a watermelon seed and that seed actually started to sprout and grow into a full-size watermelon over the course of a few weeks. The pain slowly grew more intense.

The day I was taken to the doctor was the day I couldn't even stand up straight. I made it through the full day of school and the bus ride home. The walk from the bus stop to my house is when the pain hit so hard I felt like I was about to die on the street. I crawled home, dragging myself on my knees with one hand holding my intestines in and one hand to the ground for balance. I made it through the front door but not much farther. Luckily, we made it to the hospital before my appendix burst. I remember the doctor telling us if we were a minute later into surgery, I would not have made it. By some miracle, my appendix held on just long enough for the surgeons to safely take it out of my body. I had escaped death for the third time in my life, and I was only twelve years old.

The ocean always fascinated me and still does. Anytime I went to the beach, I had to go in the water and battle with the waves. I always feel a special connection with the ocean even when standing alongside it. I have come to believe that all life-forms on this planet can trace its ancestry to the ocean. Science has proven that the first life-form originated from the ocean as a single-celled organism. Water is ancient and magical, more powerful than we can comprehend. And on this particular day, I found out just how powerful the ocean is.

It was a hot summer morning, and my family and I decided to go to one of the local beaches on the south shore. I remember the waves were very tall that day, and I was looking forward to facing them head-on. The sound of crashing waves against the shore and the mist on my face was calling me to come and play. I was a teenager and full of expendable energy. I dove right in, tackling the next wave that grew toward me. My favorite spot was right at the moment where the tip of a tall wave came barreling down, crashing into the tide traveling back toward the ocean and causing a huge splash. This crash point is where I would bend my knees, lower my shoulders, and lunge forward with my feet never really leaving the sand. I tested my strength against the strength of the crashing waves. Sometimes I stood my ground, and sometimes I got knocked off my feet. I loved either outcome. My joy was the battle itself, not the outcome of the battle.

After getting knocked around a few times, I swam past the crash point and would bodysurf the waves onto the shore. Even though this activity was exhilarating for me, it was also exhausting. I usually knew when to take a break and lie back down on my towel a couple feet away from the ocean's tide to catch my breath. But on this day, I battled with the ocean one wave too many. I remember getting hit so hard by a wave that I was not only knocked off my feet but I was also thrown and then pulled several feet laterally down into the current and back into the ocean past the waves. I was disoriented, exhausted, out of breath, and underwater. I swam up as hard as I could to reach the surface. When I finally made it above the sea level, I looked around to see if I could recognize where my family was sitting so I could call out for help. But I didn't recognize anything or anyone on shore. I was thrown so far laterally that my family was no longer in my line of sight.

I started to panic because I was having trouble paddling to stay above the water. Then an unexpected wave came crashing down on top of me, sending me back down toward the depths of the sea. Now I was truly scared. I had to get back onto shore or I was sure to drown. I started paddling straight toward the shore, but at this point, I was not strong enough to swim against the riptide that kept pulling me back out to sea. The most important thing I needed to do was to catch my breath, so I did my best paddling to stay in one spot to keep my head above the water. I was no longer fighting against the current, and I noticed something started to happen. If I didn't try to swim, the current would move me back and forth but also a little to the right. Instead of paddling straight, I started paddling to the right and, at the same time, tried to utilize the force of the waves to push me forward. I realized it was easier to move in a diagonal direction toward the shore as opposed to directly straight toward the shore.

Slowly but surely and without going against the grain too much, my feet finally met with the sand. Staggering and gasping for air, I made it to the point where my feet were no longer in the water and were only touching the sand. I collapsed right there and must have laid in the sand for a good fifteen minutes before I gained the strength to stand again. By some miracle, a primal instinct to survive kicked in and I went with the flow that saved my life. Thank God because as I looked around, no one seemed to even notice that I had been face-to-face with death just a few moments ago.

The second car I owned was a used dark-blue 1994 Camaro. I loved that car and that time period of my life. This was when I had developed a large and widespread clientele from selling weed. We went to house parties, bars, and clubs just about every night of the week. I made alliances, acquaintances, drinking buddies, and friends who only cared about having a good time. Everything else in life was secondary. I drove all around Long Island and the eastern parts of the city in that car. Camaros are fast, but the rear-wheel drive does not do very well in the snow.

It was the later part of the afternoon, and I was driving home from work during rush hour in a snowstorm. As I started to merge onto the highway from the service road, my car started to fishtail. I tried to gain control of the wheel, but the back of the car was swerving too far in both directions. I turned the wheel too hard in the opposite direction of the fishtail, and the back end of my car went from a fishtail into complete full spins in the right lane of the highway. It felt like a full two-and-a-half rotations. By the time I was done spinning, I was facing the opposite direction of traffic and was on the shoulder of the highway.

I sat there in the driver's seat in shock, in complete confusion and disbelief of what just happened. By some miracle, I spun down the highway and onto the shoulder instead of oncoming traffic, maybe because of the curvature of the road. Either way, I had been facing a certain catastrophe and then had narrowly escaped death. I waited a long time for a big enough separation in the traffic for me to make a U-turn back onto the highway, and then I proceeded home at a speed no faster than 20 MPH.

I got shot at on a drug deal gone wrong. Paul and I were in a bad neighborhood trying to score drugs from people we did not know. We were desperate, and none of our usual dealers were around that night. We couldn't find heroin anywhere else, so we decided to venture into the "bad part of town." Paul and I met through my good friend Mike M. who I spent the later part of high school with break-dancing. Mike went to an Upstate New York college, and I went to a local state college. We were forced to go our separate ways, but we met back up when school was out. During our college years, we both experimented heavily with drugs and brought our habits back home with us. Our relationship became toxic because when he wanted to take a break, I wanted to get high. When I wanted to take a break, he wanted to get high. This high probability caused us never to be able to take a break.

Mike was a little more outspoken than me when it came to drugs. He was not conservative and did not care who knew he was high and that he had plenty of cocaine for sale. It devastated me when he was taken to jail for selling four ounces of cocaine to an undercover cop right outside our apartment. When he came back home from jail after a year, Mike brought back a friend with him and introduced him into our circle. This was how I met Paul, and I found out very quickly that Paul was more careless and reckless than me and Mike combined. At first, I loved that quality about him, and that's why Paul and I were friends for the next few years to follow.

We were now driving around North Bellport in the middle of the night looking for anyone on the street who we could ask to help us find heroin. Looking back now, I can clearly see how stupid this was. But at the time, this was the best idea we ever had. We were on the lookout for a new twenty-four-hour drug dealer. We called out to the first form of life we came across. He agreed to help us, and we let him into the car. He instructed us to drive around the block a few times until he got in touch with the dealer. We gave him our money, and he had us stop just outside the light between two streetlamps. He got out of the car and proceeded down the driveway of a house that had no cars, no lights, and no sign of life inside. I quietly whispered to Paul, "This doesn't feel right, bro. Let's just get out of here. I know of another dealer a couple miles away."

Paul insisted, "No way, bro. I just gave that guy all my money. Plus, I'm sick. We need this dope right now. Fuck it, we're right here. Just chill."

Still with a terrible feeling in my gut, I let Paul know my plan. "I am keeping the car in drive with my foot on the break. Open the door on your side, and leave it open. Do not get too far from the car when these guys come out and start to approach us. This should be a very simple hand off because we already gave them the money. But if anything is in their hands other than the drugs, you dive headfirst into this fucking car and I'm speeding off! You got it?"

I could tell Paul was a little nervous, too, as he whispered back, "Yeah, bro. I got it." After a long nerve-racking wait, they finally came out of that house. Paul opened his passenger-side door and let them approach us. I heard them greet each other quietly, but then their conversation started to trail off. I couldn't hear what was being said. One of the guys started behaving aggressively. He took a big step toward Paul and spoke through his teeth, "What you say?" This was an obvious cue for us to get the fuck out of there.

I leaned toward Paul's direction and yelled, "Paul, get back in the car." Once they heard me signal to Paul, a handgun was drawn. I screamed to Paul again, "Paul, get back in the fucking car now!" Paul literally dove headfirst into the car, and with the passenger door still open, I slammed on the gas pedal. As the car went from zero to a hundred, we heard gunshots go off. I swerved left and right slightly as to create a moving target and made the first possible turn onto a cross street. I hoped and prayed that would be the first and last time I would ever get shot at. By some miracle, those bullets missed me, Paul, and my car.

The closest I have come to actually dying was my first heroin overdose. My family and I went on vacation to Mexico with our neighbors one summer while I was still relatively new to heroin and my addiction had not yet become an everyday habit. So being away from it for seven days didn't drive me completely insane. We had the all-inclusive deal, so drinks were free all day and all night. Obviously, I was completely hammered the entire trip. The time away from my everyday environment was a nice change of pace for me. Plus, I was completely entertained with all the fun and excitement that the Mexican resort and dance clubs had to offer. After many new and amazing memories were made, it was time to head back home.

By the time we got back to New York, it was somewhere around midnight. I could have gone to bed, but I decided to stay up and try to find some dope. I was back in my everyday environment, my week-long drunken buzz had worn off, and my cravings for drugs started to creep in. This might not make sense to some, but not being high in this moment just didn't feel right, and I was determined to make it right and throw my very own homecoming party. To my surprise, one of my dealers answered the phone, and we agreed on a meeting spot about twenty minutes away from where I was. I waited for everyone to go to bed, then I snuck out the back door to go meet up with him. I drove quickly and carefully, picked up the dope, then flew back home. I waited until I got back home to open the bags.

At first, I shot two bags and enjoyed the ride. I turned on the computer in our living room to see if anyone was online I could flirt with. At this time, everyone in the house had settled in and gone to sleep. I was feeling good, but it had been so long since I felt this high that I wanted to get a little higher. The time away from using drugs had lowered my tolerance a lot, and I was feeling the full effect with a very low dose. I had a cigarette, and not even ten minutes later, I was fiending for more, mostly because I had a couple more bags in my pocket.

I locked the bathroom door behind me and set everything up to shoot another two bags. I pushed the sink drain down and turned on the faucet to make a little bath I could clean my needle with. I sucked the clean water from the sink into the needle, then pushed it out into the toilet. I repeated this process three times to ensure a clean needle, free from my blood and the cut from the last use. I bit off a small piece of cotton from a new Q-tip, chewed it into a small ball, then placed it into the plunger cap. Carefully, I removed the tape from the dope bags that held them shut. I ripped off the top section of the bag that the tape was attached to and set them aside onto a dry surface of the countertop. Then I took out a dollar bill from my wallet and folded down the center, longways.

I dumped the dope from both bags onto the creased bill, pinched one end of the bill, then carefully shook the dope to the pinched end of the bill. Using the dollar bill as a funnel, I poured the dope into the cap where the little cotton ball was waiting. I sucked up the clean water from the sink to fill about three-quarters of the needle. Then I gently squirted the clean water into the heroin-filled cap, making sure to hit the side of the cap as to not cause the powder to jump out. I pulled out the plunger from the needle to use it as muddler. I mixed the water and heroin thoroughly then put the plunger back into the needle. With the point of the needle, I found the cotton at the bottom of the brown heroin water. Gently, I pushed against the cotton and sucked up the diluted heroin slowly.

At the time, the inner crease of my left elbow was my go-to spot. I hit the vein every time. I slowly pushed the needle into my favorite vein. Surprisingly, this part does not hurt. That is, of course, if I am using a new needle. I pulled back on the plunger just a little bit to make sure blood entered the needle, letting me know for sure that the tip of the needle is inside my vein and not outside. Finally, I eased the heroin into my bloodstream. The high hit me in three seconds.

I cleaned everything up then sat back down at the computer. My fingers hit the keyboard, and that's the last thing I remember. I had overdosed for the first time. I was dying. And then the strangest thing started to happen. I felt a sensation of floating up toward the ceiling. I was no longer in my body. Only my consciousness started floating up toward the ceiling, and I was able to look down at my body. What I witnessed was both of my parents on their knees in front of my lifeless body. I couldn't tell exactly what was going on, but I knew something was wrong. Floating away didn't feel right, so I moved closer toward my body. My eyes started to open.

The first thing I felt was a set of hands gripping my shoulders. My dad was violently shaking me. Then the next thing I realized was something cold and damp on my forehead. My mom was patting my forehead and face with a damp cloth. Then the reality of the situation and my memories came back to me. I remembered what I had just done and also realized that my parents were frantically trying to bring me back to life. I can only imagine their disbelief and confusion. As I laid there on my back, I looked around the room and saw my younger brother and sisters were there too. So was an EMT, a fireman, and a police officer.

When I saw the cop, I almost jumped out of my skin. I thought my pockets had been searched and that he was waiting to arrest me. I cannot describe the look of disbelief in my siblings' eyes. The EMT wanted to take me away, but I refused the medical attention. I insisted that I was fine, but my parents then took charge and made me get on the stretcher and into the ambulance. I was so embarrassed. Later that night, my mom explained more of the details to their side of this story. My brother was in his room, which was right next to the living room where I was. He heard the thump of my body hitting the floor when I fell back in the computer chair. My brother found me lying there, lifeless and turning blue. Then he rushed upstairs to wake up my parents to tell them that there was something wrong with me. By the grace of God, he was still awake and heard me hit the floor then had the curiosity to investigate. If no one heard me fall that night, I would not be here today. My brother was the one who saved my life that night. I am graciously forever in debt to him.

Getting bullied and constantly picked on is not a near-death experience, but after a while of putting up with that kind of torture, it made me want to kill someone or myself. Especially when one starts to consider and believe what the bullies are saying. Teasing and kidding around among friends is fun, and in many circles, it's encouraged. It is not fun when the jabs and stabs are focused on your weaknesses and experienced daily. I have been made fun of for just being myself at every stage of my life. It seems that in every new environment I am placed, there is an antagonizing bully I have to deal with. If I liked to do things a little different and express my uniqueness, I got made fun of. If I was quiet and stayed to myself, I got made fun of. If I did well in school because I did my homework and studied, I got made fun of. If I look a little different than every-one else, I got made fun of.

I was bullied in my new elementary school for being new.

I was bullied in junior high for being quiet and the smart one in class.

I was bullied in high school for doing my own thing and start-ing a break-dancing club.

I was bullied at work for being a rookie and being unsure of what to do.

I was bullied at work for having obvious potential that was seen as a threat to the senior guys.

The act of committing suicide was looking very good because of the amount of torment that I had endured. I was desperate for an escape, desperate for these terrible people to be taken out of my life. By the grace of God, I did not go through with it. I do believe that my desire to escape reality can be directly traced to the daily bullying I dealt with for years along with a severe heartbreak followed by my dreams being crushed and unrealized. These were also causes for my desire to escape my reality.

Bullies achieve satisfaction by making other people feel small and inadequate. There must come a point when you have had enough and take action to make the bullying stop. You have to show the bully you're not afraid. Never cower or make yourself small to make other people feel better. If you are good at what you do, there will always be people who are not as talented who will envy you. Do not feel bad for these people who envy. Instead, try to offer your assistance in some way. Attempt to form an alliance or, at the very least, reach an agreement to stay out of each other's way. The idea here is to share your talent or even teach something. We must figure out a way to use our powers for good and to not keep them all to ourselves. If there are still people who hate you for being talented, stay away from them. Some people are only happy when they see other people fail.

Some bullies just don't know when to quit. There are some people that just cannot be reasoned with. And I have a message for them. This is for every single bully that I have come across in my life. This is for every single person who tried to pull me down and wished failure upon me.

Why Must Bullies Be Put in My Path?

To make me stronger. The bullies' actions all stem from fear. They're afraid I'm going to take their job, but I know they would never admit it. But I don't need the admission. I see right through them. Behind every bully is a scared little boy. I see them tremble. They see how good I am, and it scares them. Don't worry. I don't want your job. It's a bullshit title anyway. You can stop trying to find dirt on me because I'm squeaky clean. You won't be able to get shit on me! You'll be working for me some day. Time is on my side, old man. And I'm watching you destroy yourself a little more each day.

Go ahead and keep obsessing over me. Watch me constantly improve. I know your envy is your poison. Go ahead and take another sip. I just stabbed you in the heart because I want you to feel yourself bleed to death. I don't need you to like me. I need you to respect me and get the fuck out of my way! Enough! Back off! What's your problem? Why are you so obsessed with me? I know exactly what I am doing. I don't need you micromanaging me and picking apart everything I do to try to find something wrong with it. No one does what I do better than me. Stop yelling at me for doing my fucking job! You know what? Go ahead and yell. Tire yourself out, you miserable bastard. You don't even faze me. Your words mean nothing to me. Go ahead and obsess over me. I'm everything you wish you were. All you're doing is making me stronger.

(The above paragraph is a letter I wrote but never sent. I have learned that this is a healthy way to let out my emotions out without hurting or disturbing anyone. Letting out my anger and frustration in this way takes a heavy weight off my back. I suggest giving it a try if you feel it is necessary.)

Respect...it is our God-given responsibility. You don't have to like the person that is giving you a hard time. But you have to do your best to respect them. The difficult experience they are putting you through is making you stronger, whether you recognize it or not. Also keep in mind that the person yelling at you is also yelling at themselves. This could be for a few subconscious reasons. They see something in you that they wish they had. They see something different from them, or they see something in you that they also see in themselves that they do not like. They are probably having a difficult moment in their lives. That's why they are being such a bitch.

So try not to take it too personal. I know it's difficult not to take it personal. But they are hurting themselves much more than they are hurting you. See through their shitty attitude. See the scared little boy or girl inside them. Because that's what's driving their insecurities and harsh, condescending tone. Try to find empathy for them, without them knowing it.

Why do bad things happen to good people? In general, we must go through war to experience peace. We can't enjoy the sunshine without the rain. We would not know happiness without sadness. We would not understand good without bad. One cannot exist without the other. Opposites attract and also keep the universe in balance. We all walk upon the duplicitous edge of life and death every day.

We are on one hell of a journey, an uphill path in life. If you are improving all aspects of your life, you are moving upward. Going up is much harder than going down. I think we all can relate to that. The uphill battle is not an easy ride, but it's worth every step. Plan ahead, and be well prepared for the next day.

I do my homework and study for the test, but I still have to deal with adversity and solve problems every day. Life is not easy. It never was, and it may never be. That's why so few make it to the metaphorical top. There are millions of people with dreams of obtaining the fame and fortune of rock stars and movie stars. How many actually make it there? The answer is very few. Unless you are born into a wealthy family, you have your work cut out for you. It is no secret that the rich stay rich by keeping the poor staying poor. But it is also no secret that if you work your ass off and dedicate the majority of your time to reaching your goals, eventually, you will get there. The most difficult part of working hard to reach your goals is having patience. Patience with your own self-improvement. Patience with other people and their inability to notice your skills or their complete ignoring of your skills and accomplishments.

What about tragedy? During our lifetime, there is a high probability of experiencing tragedy. If something terrible happens to someone you love, the most important thing to do is to be there for them. Provide as much support as you can and show them that you do not want them to face this challenge alone. Tragedies are difficult enough to deal with; it is more difficult to deal with them alone. The message I am trying to convey is "Look out for one another." The Bible asks us to "Love thy neighbor." If every single person assisted the person behind them, the world would be in a much better place than it is now. If you are going through a personal tragedy, the one thing not to do is avoid and run away. The longer the pain is ignored and left untreated, the longer it will remain. Everyone loves someone. If I ease you through your pain, it is only natural that you will want to ease me through my pain.

CHAPTER 9

A CLEAN SLATE

Returning to winter break of my senior year of college, I had finally reached a point in my life where I was ready to give rehab a try. I had beaten myself up past the point of exhaustion. I had enough of creating hell for myself. My feelings toward rehab were optimistic and skeptical at the same time. But there were a lot of underlying problems within my psyche. When I take the time to try and remember all the terrible things that have happened to me over the years, I can't believe I'm still alive. I can't believe I continued going through life ignoring all this bullshit. I started out as such an innocent kid, then my life seemed to get more difficult as time went on.

By the age of twenty-nine, I had escaped all my enemies, but I was still running from them in my mind. The reality I was creating for myself was unbearable. I was almost thirty years old and felt like I hadn't really accomplished anything with my life. I spent all my time and money on partying, going to bars and clubs, getting drugs, and getting tattoos. I had met a lot of pretty girls, but none of those relationships lasted more than a few months. If the music and atmosphere were right, I could break-dance, but that didn't lead me anywhere.

I was the lead singer of a kick-ass rock band for a couple of years, but we were never offered a record deal. I'd been drawing and abstract painting just about my entire life and had not sold one painting. None of my talents were taking me anywhere, and they definitely were not making me any money. So it was very difficult to feel proud about them. The only thing I had going for me at the time was that I was in my senior year of college. If rehab went well during this winter break, I only had one more semester left until graduating in the spring of 2013.

But who was I? This question haunted me for years. The only thing I had known was chasing the next high. That's what my life had felt like since the beginning. It was always me chasing something that was very far away or running from something that was right behind me. My entire being fell apart when I got my heart broken. I was never the same after that. Before that day, I still had a little respect for myself at least. I used to take care of my health. I used to be conscious of what I ate and drank. I had love to give my friends and family and to the world. My outlook on life was bright. Back then my general thoughts consisted of *Everything's going to be okay.* Now my lingering thoughts said, *Fuck it. What's the point of trying?* I was watching all my friends get good jobs, buy houses, and start families. And here I was still living with my parents and on my way to rehab.

I always believed I could be great one day. I knew I had the potential to be or do anything I wanted. When I really try to learn something new, I learn it. I practice until I'm satisfied with myself and the results. Nothing was ever handed to me. I earned every dollar, every material object, every relationship, every skill. But I was wasting it all. I started experimenting with drugs for the fun and excitement then ended up having to use drugs just to feel normal. If I didn't use, I would get violently sick and then go more and more insane with every passing minute. It started off as fun. It started off as a way to escape my broken heart. Anything was better than wallowing in pain and misery. But pain and misery is what I ended up creating for myself in the end anyway. I was running away from withdrawal before it even began to hit. I was chasing a high that I could never catch. I was running from a reality that just kept getting worse. Heroin takes the mental and physical pain away at first. Then when you become addicted, all it does is cause pain. At first, the high lasts all day and night. After a few years of using, the high lasts five minutes. Same goes for cocaine. I had become a hollow shell of a human. There was one ounce of life energy left inside me. One ounce of hope that I could get my life back on track.

Because of my DUI, my license had been taken away, and I was forced to apply for unemployment, which qualified me for Medicaid. Medicaid paid for my stay at Seafield Center. There was no way I could afford inpatient rehab without the help of Medicaid. During my stay at Seafield, I was forced to live three weeks clean from all substances. They weened me off the dope with Vicodin. That was amazing news for me at the time because I thought I would have to wait for the drugs to pass through my system cold turkey, which would have made me go through the torture of withdrawal for about two weeks. I would rather die than to have to go through that.

The first couple days of rehab were not that bad. The time between the Vicodin doses I was given were getting further and further apart. Weening off anything sucks. But the way Seafield got me sober was easier that I thought it would be. The Vicodin was still giving me the opiates my body craved, but it was in very small doses, which prevented me from withdrawing. After a few days, I was no longer functioning with the assistance of illegal substances for the first time in many years. With a clear body and mind, I began to feel my emotions again. I found myself crying out of nowhere. I was having realizations that my years of reckless actions had landed me in rehab, and I couldn't believe that I was actually there. Thoughts like *How did I end up here? How did I let my life get this bad?* I was going through extreme feelings of guilt and shame for the pain I had caused my family, friends, and myself.

There are very few people who are optimistic in rehab. Just about everyone in there is on their way to jail. Most people are there because they are court mandated, and they're trying to make themselves look better for the judge. If they are not battling the court for their freedom, they are battling with their family or employer for their freedom and reputation. Almost everyone has reservations of getting completely wrecked the day they get out. Anger, misery, anxiety, and depression is felt in the air all throughout the facility. It is not a pleasant place to be.

After a couple days of being sober, I started to gain a little confidence. I started to believe that I could actually stay sober. That belief had never crossed my mind before because once I started really getting heavy into drinking and drugging, I never let the buzz completely fade away. I always felt like I had to be on something to remain sane. But these three weeks staying in inpatient taught me that living completely sober was possible. My mind started to become more and more clear. I started to remember all the things that I was subconsciously blocking out for years. I started to remember all the terrible things I did to feed my habit, how I slowly ruined every relationship I had, and how lucky I was to still be alive and to still be somewhat healthy.

One of the main lessons we are taught in sobriety is "Stay sober, and carry the message of sobriety to help the next suffering alcoholic." Because of AA's widespread availability, a helping hand is not far away to anyone seeking help. I have found it to be true that the one asking for help is required to do the work necessary to stay distracted long enough to remain sober. Sobriety is not handed to you. It is earned. You get what you put into it. You have to work on improving yourself daily through talking to and assisting other alcoholics get through their pain and confusion. Then once you get a decent grip on your new way of living and understanding, it becomes your responsibly to help the next person in need in and out of the rooms of AA. Living sober requires a lot of time and attention, and it is worth every bit of it.

During the years I was living helplessly addicted to drugs and alcohol, I had become extremely selfish. The addictions became my top priority, and not by choice. I had no idea of how demanding the cravings would get. Every day, I went through the same trauma. The best way I can attempt to describe heroin withdrawal is with an analogy. Imagine waking up at the bottom of the ocean. You don't know how you got there, but this is your reality right now. You must find a way to get above the water. Immediately, you realize that you do not have a lot of time before you drown and die. Extreme panic sets in. A sense of urgency and pending doom is in the forefront. That is how I felt every morning I woke up: from a pleasant dreamland into a sudden reality where I couldn't breathe. I was kicking and gasping for air. Survival instincts kicked in immediately, and the only thing on my mind was doing whatever it took to make this panic go away. The voices in my head screamed for heroin!

It was the only thing I could hear because the screams got louder and louder as the seconds went on. Frantically, I would get dressed and rush out the door. There was no time to eat or even brush my teeth. Speeding to the closest ATM, I called my list of dealers and set up a meeting spot with the first one who answered the phone. I spent every dollar I ever had. I pawned any possession worth anything. I bargained and begged my friends for money so I could shoot heroin just to feel normal. I borrowed more money than I could pay back all the time to the point where my friends stopped answering my calls. I made countless promises to the drug dealers. I said I would pay them back the next day and never did. Every morning, I was in a state of hopeless desperation. Somehow, I always found a way to get my medicine. I became very good at manipulation. I became a great hostage negotiator. Every morning, I kicked through the dark murky ocean floor that was my life until I made it above water.

The most sought-after effect of using heroin is to just feel normal. The relief from the overwhelming panic and anxiety is what I wanted most. The waves of euphoria and a pain-free body and mind was secondary. Everything else in my life had to wait until I could breathe again.

Can you image how grateful I felt when I finally experienced a morning that I did not have to go through that? Words could not express just how lucky, just how grateful I felt during my first clean days in rehab. Now that I no longer depended on drugs to survive the day, I had plenty of time to help a fellow addict in need. There are special phrases and sayings in AA that I have come to live by, such as "You must give to the next person what was so freely given to you." This made perfect sense to me from the start because that was how I truly felt.

I completely understand the suffering that the struggling addict is going through, and now that I had been granted a taste of sobriety, I wanted all other fellow addicts to be free from their torment as well. There is a statistic that states only 4 percent of addicts and alcoholics get sober and actually stay sober. The fact that I was experiencing sobriety felt like nothing short of a miracle. There must be a divine power at work for me to be living sober. Naturally, my beliefs of God begin to awaken. I was beginning to see my life, and life in total, in an entirely bright new way.

CHAPTER 10

RELIGION 101

I grew up in a Christian Catholic family. I am 75 percent Sicilian Italian with a 25 percent mix of French, Irish, and Eastern European. Grandpa Allen, my mother's father, contributes to the 25 percent mix. The other three grandparents are from Sicily and parts of Italy. I was always proud of my heritage and respected the traditions. I participated in all traditional ceremonies that came with being a part of the Christian Catholic faith: baptism, Communion, and confirmation.

I took Grandpa Allen's name for my confirmation, Arthur. I always had so much respect for Grandpa Allen. He didn't say much, but he didn't have to. His talents and achievements spoke for them themselves. He had a full-scale master carpenter's shop in his garage. He personally took care of all the maintenance and home improvements—not just his own but all of his family's as well. I learned he was a marine in the military from the memorabilia in his house. After he completed his military service, he became a civil engineer working for the city of New York and kept that job for the remainder of his career until retirement.

On the weekends, he was the driving force of all of my aunt's and uncle's kitchen and bathroom remodels. I remember him installing all-new wood doors in our house when I was much younger. He built a tremendous exterior deck in his own backyard. He fixed plumbing leaks and repaired boilers. He built interior and exterior furniture of all kinds and built huge dollhouses for his granddaughters. The list goes on.

If he wasn't maintaining his home, he was cooking. Grandpa Allen was also an amazing cook. Now that I'm thinking back, I don't remember Grandma Allen cooking dinner much. It was always Grandpa. If he ever took a break, he would do so with his Budweiser and Camel cigarettes. The refrigerator in his garage was always stocked with Buds, top to bottom. The only thing in that fridge was beer. I always thought that was so cool. As kids, Cousin Corey and I would play with all the tools that were hanging on the wall. Our favorite thing was to grab a hammer that we liked then proceed to swing at the concrete floor in the garage. We loved to watch the concrete floor begin to crack and crumble. When we were caught destroying that concrete floor, oh my god. Grandpa lost his mind. We got screamed at, smacked around, and scared to death. When Grandpa got mad, everyone knew. Holy shit, he was a scary man when he was pushed over the edge and into madness.

How could I not look up to this man? I love him. But I never knew how to tell him or show him that. Maybe since he never really said anything, I never said anything. Besides when I was a baby, he was never affectionate with me, so I never knew how to be affectionate with him. Not even in a manly way. It was perfectly clear that he loved and cared for us all, he just didn't verbally express his love. But he did everything and more that a devoted husband and grandfather could do. I feared him, I was intimidated by him, but I loved him more. I watched him closely because I admired him so much. I believe I learned a strong work ethic from him. I inherited his laser-beam focus and his blue eyes. He was, and still is, a great man. Nothing can take that away from him. Not even death. Often, I pray to him, and I ask him to grant me his strength, his wisdom, his courage, and for him to continue to guide me in the right direction. I truly believe that he is close to me and hears my prayers.

Grandpa Rizzo was the first grandparent I started praying to because he was the first one to cross over to the other side. I was two years old when he passed, so I never really got a chance to meet him. The only memories I have of him are from pictures that have been given to me by my aunt and uncles. They have told me so many amazing stories about him that I feel as if I really do know him. The loving stories I have been told about him only make me admire him even more. I have always loved Grandpa Rizzo and always will. Often, I pray to him and ask for his protection, guidance, and for his ability to love.

Was I religious? I don't know. Kind of. Metaphorically, I always had one foot in the holy water and one foot out. I always believed in a god. Or at least believed that there was something more ancient and powerful at work in our universe. I knew that there was no big bearded man in the sky. Even as a kid, I knew that was a metaphor. I knew not to take the stories in the Bible too literally. I could see that there was a moral to the story and that the book was trying to teach us how to live together as one united people.

I also saw the corruption within the history of the religion and how the church was the government in its beginning. I could see how the church used fear to manipulate their followers to do what they were told. This is the main reason why I never fully dove into religion. But as I got older, I started looking for more truthful answers to life's difficult questions, my questions. It took many years of trial and error for me to see that my ideas and way of life was not working.

During my first attempt at living sober, I was desperate for answers. Christianity only took me so far. At first glance, Jesus's words are a bunch of riddles. I needed to hear something that got straight to the point. Right after I got out of rehab, I attended AA meetings on a regular basis. I was learning more about how to live than I did while attending church. On the weekends, I would go to the local bookstore as my continued search for finding a magical book with all the answers. Even though I now had a clear mind and body, my confusion and misunderstanding of life and how to live still remained.

CHAPTER 11

WHEN CONFUSION TURNS INTO FRUSTRATION WHICH TURNS INTO RAGE

It is important for me to note that the following venting was a result of years of suppressed emotions, years of feeling like I was being held back from accelerating in my life. Because I started using drugs around when I was nineteen years old, I was never able to mentally mature past nineteen years old. By the time I completed rehab, I was twenty-nine. As the fog began to clear in my mind, I started to realize that I was ten years behind schedule. I watched many of my friends graduate from college, start good careers, buy houses, start a family, and save their money for retirement. Then here I was at twenty-nine years old, and I still hadn't completed enough schooling to get a decent job. In reality, the one thing that had been holding me back was me. And that was becoming more and more obvious. That is my definition of frustration.

Tell 'Em Why You're Mad!

Nothing makes sense. We were meant for more than this! Why do I feel like we're all slaves? Life was promised to be magical and awesome, and it turned out to be all a lie! Everything sucks. Everyone is an asshole. No one gives a fuck.

What's the fucking point? I might as well stay high. We're all going to die anyway. I was told I could be anything I want to be. Bullshit! I have to lie, cheat, and steal to get to where I want to be. I'm told NO everywhere I go. I can't tell what's real anymore. Is money even real? It's man-made, made by the government. And we're told that our value is determined by how much of this paper we have.

Beautiful women don't hang out with poor men. By the time you're twenty-five, you better be well on your way to becoming a millionaire. If not, you're a loser and are going nowhere in life. We're told to change and change and change. Be better, get better, try harder, keep trying. Every morning I wake up and ask myself, "Why do I have to keep doing this?" I have to say to myself, "Fuck it. I guess I'll keep doing this." I've made it to twenty-nine years old, and I'm welcoming death. I'm no longer afraid to die. This life is a pain in the ass.

Everything sucks. Everything hurts. I feel like I'm losing my mind. I'm psychotic every time I wake up. I hate waking up. I hate leaving dreamland and returning to reality. Everyone and everything in life expects me to pay higher and higher prices to continue to live. My fucking bills get bigger and bigger each year. And it's not easy to make more money.

I'm sick of starting over again and again. I feel like I can never get ahead. Something always comes up and takes all my savings. That's fucking bullshit! But it is my fault? Am I the sole creator of my destiny? Am I the only one choosing my consequences? Making more money takes forever. How the fuck am I going to make more money? This is why I emulated the drug dealers I saw in the movies. I loved how they said, "Fuck the rules. I'm taking what I want."

You know what, it's cool when you're young. But once you hit twenty-five, it's not cool anymore. You have to start figuring out how to play by the rules while at the same time trying to make your dreams a reality. My family isn't rich. I couldn't ask my dad for a million-dollar loan to get my career started. I'm starting from zero. Actually, every time I try something new, I'm starting in the negative: already in debt. And no one wants to give me a shot without prior experience because I have no experience. But how do I get experience if you don't give me a shot? Goddammit!

I have to make something out of nothing. Over and over again. But my something keeps disappearing. Either I lose it or it gets taken away. Or I spend it all. Whatever it is, I have yet to be able to continue to grow a fortune. What the fuck am I doing wrong?

CHAPTER 12

STARTING OVER, AGAIN

Here I was again, trying to make something out of nothing. I was a few days fresh out of rehab. I was confident and scared at the same time. I was optimistic and doubtful, and at the same time, I wanted to do the right thing. But I was not sure if I was capable. This was mainly because I'd been living illegally for the past decade. Obviously, I needed a job. So I called up one of my previous employers who worked on home improvements all throughout Long Island. The crazy thing was when I was working with him, I was high all the time. And if I wasn't high, I was in a silent rage because I wasn't high.

Eddy picked up on that character trait immediately. Eddy was also a recovering addict and had been sober about four years when I first met him. On the first time around being employed by him, I was a mess. I called out sick late in the morning one day, and he fired me right then. He was just waiting for me to do something irresponsible to let me go. But now he was giving me a second chance. I believe he paid me the same amount per day that I was making previously with him. I think it was $120 per day, which made me excited to get started. Obviously, I was very grateful, and I showed my gratitude by working my ass off for him. Anything he asked for, I was all over it. No complaining, no hesitating. Just working.

Once you learn the techniques of a skilled trade, you never forget how to get things done. My first couple weeks working with Eddy were tough. I was the helper to everyone on the jobsite. I had to clean up everyone's mess. And being the helper, of course, everyone talked shit and fucked with me. I just kept my head down and did what I was supposed to do. The projects we were working on were big. Big enough to keep us working for about two months on each job. We added entire floors to homes, making them taller and more modern. We remodeled huge kitchens and bathrooms. We built decks, installed new windows and doors, reroofed houses, and repainted the entire interior of homes. Painting takes forever, by the way. We did it all.

I was a pretty good carpenter when I started with Eddy. By the time I left, I was a master carpenter. I watched the other workers come and go. They were hired and fired while I was leading the way in the construction operations. I started as the helper then after one year of kicking ass, Eddy made me the lead foreman.

Anyway, I was a couple months sober and developing a relationship with a new girlfriend. I met her in rehab while writing letters to each other because we would get in trouble if we got caught talking (otherwise known as fraternizing). I graduated first, and I kept writing to her while she was still in there. Mary graduated about a week after me, and we made plans to meet at her place because living at your parents' house at age twenty-nine was not cool. After a few months, I convinced her to allow me to move in with her. She lived in Roslyn, New York. Rich-people town. I really felt out of place there. Rich people can sense the poor. I see it on their face when I walk by.

But Mary was good for me. She was a few years older than me and had seen a lot more of the world than I had. She was serious about her sobriety, which made me really want to stay sober too. We went to meetings together and basically did everything together. She was fighting to get her driver's license back because of her multiple DWIs, and I had just bought a new pickup truck that I was able to buy with my new job money. So I was the one that had to drive her everywhere.

At first, I didn't mind, but after a while she started getting very impatient with me. Sometimes I was a little late picking her up because I had my own shit to take care of and had my own responsibilities. She would accuse me of cheating on her or going to bars. Basically, she was convinced I was deceiving her in some way. But I wasn't. I was 100 percent faithful to her, and I was living sober. After a couple months of being tortured by her constant accusations of cheating on her and claiming I was getting high, I started wishing for an escape. And an escape presented itself soon after me seeking it. Eddy's brother-in-law was getting Percocet on a regular basis, and I found a way to introduce myself.

CHAPTER 13

RELAPSE

I had so much going for me. I was clean and sober after about a decade under the influence. My dependence of drugs and alcohol were gone, and I was so proud of that. What I had not realized yet is how much harder it would be to get sober again. That is a hard truth that every alcoholic and addict must understand and accept.

During my first few months of newly found sobriety, getting sober for the first time seemed like an easy task. But on the way to the inpatient program, I was terrified. I was shaking like a leaf. Although I knew it was the right thing to do, I was mostly afraid of what would happen to me. I was afraid of a severe withdrawal, which would include me constantly throwing up, a complete breakdown of my nervous system, extreme hot and cold flashes, severe anxiety, severe depression, and total and complete insanity. I was afraid of a withdrawal so bad that I would rather die than to experience it for more than five minutes. Luckily, the inpatient program weened me off opiates in such a way where my withdrawal was minimal. But without a doubt, inpatient is the best way to go as the first step toward getting sober.

The real work began when I was put back into my everyday environment. My insecurities, selfishness, and fears took control again; and I was left with the consequences. Why did I think getting sober again would be easy? Knowing what I know now, I would have made different choices back then. But I wouldn't be who I am now if I hadn't made those bad choices and then learned from them. So it's difficult to be certain if I regret the past. Who would I be today if I had stayed sober starting from age twenty-nine and started developing healthy habits then? What I consider healthy habits today are much more beneficial for me and everyone around me compared to what I thought was "the right thing" back then.

Looking back on my life, I can clearly see my mistakes. But instead of wishing I had never made those mistakes and beating myself up, I have learned from those mistakes. I have learned what to do and what not to do. I have learned how to go with the flow of life as opposed to trying to force my way through life. I have learned how to be more accepting of my life and the world around me. I have learned that I am only able to change a small percentage of the world around me and that I am mostly responsible for the world within me. In short, I have much more wisdom now. So don't regret the past. Learn from it and become stronger and wiser from your real-life experiences.

During my first few months of sobriety, a true psychic change had not happened yet. The full psychic change is the point you reach when everything clicks into place. Life begins to make sense. This is when you can see your past without regretting it. You can look at your present reality and totally accept it for what it is while at the same time being optimistic about your future because you start to recognize the rate at which your life is improving. You truly believe and trust that if you do the right thing, everything will naturally fall into place. This psychic change began with my acceptance that I am indeed an addict and an alcoholic and that I can no longer drink.

My previous view on drugs and alcohol was that it was medicine, it made me stronger and more talented. Now my view on drugs and alcohol is that it is poison. Once I take the first drink, I begin a steep decline toward death. The single most-damaging thought I could ever have is *Maybe I could just do a little bit and be okay.* This thought was where my relapses began every time. My relapses began with me thinking or believing that I could drink one beer or get a little high and not be consumed by the addiction and the obsession of doing more. But that thought is the furthest thing from the truth. It is the complete opposite of the truth. That thought is my alcoholism trying to convince me to take a sip of beer, knowing that the sip leads to me drinking and drugging myself to death.

Have you experienced the psychic change within your sobriety yet? It is brought about from completing Step 1 at 100 percent. Which is saying "We admit we are powerless over alcohol—that our lives have become unmanageable." By completing this step, you first admit and accept that you are an alcoholic or addict. No more denial about this fact. You admit and accept that your life is unmanageable while under the influence. To put it another way, once you start to use drugs and alcohol, you are no longer in control of yourself and your life.

You must also accept that now that you know and understand this about yourself, you will no longer use drugs and alcohol. No more reservations on thinking or planning that maybe one day in the future you can use again. This is your surrender. You are surrendering this battle with drugs to win the war on your life. This is the choice you make of life over death, and you make a promise to yourself and to God that you will consciously make this choice of life over death every morning you wake up. That promise to yourself is the most important promise of all.

Step 1 is only one sentence, but you can write an entire book on the depth that Step 1 truly is. Step 1 is the most important step. If you cannot complete Step 1, sobriety will be a tremendous challenge for you. But if you can complete it, and it doesn't happen overnight by the way, your freedom and your life becomes more available to you. Please do not misunderstand; sobriety is earned. You can't just say, "I want to be sober now." You must talk with another experienced alcoholic who has steady sobriety in their life. Some people call it work. They say, "Sobriety takes a lot of work." But the truth is sobriety involves one basic action: surrendering.

Within your surrender, denial disappears, and optimism appears. Yes, in early sobriety you must spend most of your time keeping yourself distracted from your old habits. You do this by going to meetings, spending time with other alcoholics, and talking to people that are just like you. During these conversations, you both begin to tell your story of how you got here. Why you think you got here, how it got started, how to remain sober, and your plans for the future. You both begin to truly relate to one another on a deep emotional level, and it is a beautiful process. Connecting with another alcoholic on an emotional level is an amazing experience, and it never gets old.

I believe all humans crave an emotional connection with another human being. For some alcoholics, this will be the first time an emotional connection is felt. And the connection makes you want to continue this new relationship. Continuing with going deeper into Step 1, you must now believe that drugs and alcohol are poison for you. We can accept it may work for some people. But not for us. We used to have a belief that drugs and alcohol were the answer that solved our problems. That they made us stronger, smarter, and just overall better. You must now truly BELIEVE, not think, that drugs and alcohol only hurt us and everyone close to us. Because that is truly the truth.

We can reminisce about "the good ol' days," but that is in the past. And that's where it will stay. It is up to us to create a beautiful future for ourselves and everyone close to us and to become the great men and women we were always destined to become. This beautiful future will naturally unfold just as long as we keep drugs and alcohol out of our lives. This is completing Step 1 at 100 percent. It is now a belief that we believe with every cell in our body. We accept and believe that using drugs and alcohol in any way will only hurt us and everyone around us. This psychic change will not only improve our lives but also every other life that we come in contact with. Believe and have faith. Everything will be okay as long as we do the right thing. Everything will naturally fall into place. All dreams and goals are now possible.

Getting back to my first relapse before anyone taught me any of this valuable information: by this point, I had read many spiritual and self-help books, and I was absorbing all the information. But I wasn't practicing it in life. A famous prayer in AA is the Serenity Prayer: "God, grant me the serenity to accept the things I cannot change, courage to change the things I can, and wisdom to know the difference."

With Mary's jealousy and constant demands, I was able to accept her for who she was, but I did not have the courage to change certain aspects that I did not like. Instead, I ran away from my problems and frustrations. I clenched my teeth and forced my way through our relationship instead of having a productive conversation with her to agree on a compromise. Forcing my way through life takes a heavy toll on me. It slowly wears me down until I break. Then when my patience wears out, I snap into a psychotic breakdown.

I no longer agree to "play by the rules." That's the point when I say, "Fuck it, time to get high. At least there I am happy." Subconsciously, I know it's the wrong thing to do. A thick blanket of denial covers my every thought and action, and I find a way to get the drugs. I'm satisfied for a few short hours, but then eventually, I have to go back home to the reality I originally attempted to escape from. So all that stress and all that work brought me right back to where I started. But now I was also in debt to my sobriety and sanity. Then the process repeats the next day. Instead of facing my problems and taking the necessary actions to make them go away or at least make them smaller, I go out and get high to avoid having to do that.

In reality, it's a lot less work to just tell the truth about how I feel. But at that point in my life, I was still battling my uncompromising ego. My ego had too much pride and would not allow me to bend for another person. Not even for those I loved and honestly cared for. In my early days of sobriety, I was not able to recognize when my ego kicked in and prevented me from doing the right thing. Today, my ego is still active, but now I am able to recognize its negative thinking. I am able to recognize negative thoughts and then challenge them. Challenging negative thoughts involves recognizing them as being negative thoughts. Realize that your brain produces negative thoughts on its own. When the thought appears, try to figure out where it came from. Did it come from your ego's selfishness? Did it come from your ego's fear? Did it come from your ego's insecurities and uncertainties?

Just recognize this process that takes place within you. If you can just witness this process without judging yourself and also without acting upon or following through with the negative thought, it will begin to get smaller. Eventually, it will disappear. As the negative thought gets smaller because of your witnessing without action, a new positive thought begins to form. You will know it's a positive thought because it will feel correct. It will feel like the right thing to do within every cell of your being. It's otherwise known as "going with your gut" as opposed to going with that first thought in your mind.

The mind is an amazing creation. It has been designed to protect us and keep us from danger. The mind is always trying to fix things. Sometimes you can find it trying to fix things in your past as well as the future. The mind has a difficult time staying in the present moment. And if you are not aware of what your mind is trying to do, it can lead you to some pretty uncomfortable places. As I have come to find out.

Isn't it funny how history repeats itself? Isn't it crazy how karma comes back around? What goes in must come out. What goes up must come down. For every action, there is an equal but opposite reaction. Mary was jealous, impatient, and doubtful of me the same way I was jealous, envious, and doubtful of Desiree. The tables had turned, and know I could clearly see what it was like to be the defendant. It was exhausting defending myself constantly. Exhausting and frustrating.

It was so annoying that I started taking Percocet once in a while to make my frustration go away. That "once in a while" turned into "all the time." Then when I couldn't get the pills, I would seek out the heroin. Slowly but surely, heroin crept into my everyday life again. The fighting in my relationship with Mary became too much for me to tolerate. I could no longer continue a relationship with someone who constantly accused me of things I was not doing.

I moved back into my parents' house for a few months to save up enough money to move out and get a place of my own again. I found an affordable studio apartment in Forest Hills, Queens. I was so happy to be by myself with no one to watch over me or tell me what to do. My only piece of furniture was a futon that folded from a couch to a bed, and I loved it. All I needed was my futon and the TV.

After work, I picked up some snacks at the grocery store, dinner from the Spanish or Chinese restaurant, and a beer or two from the deli. I was in heaven. I was a bachelor again in my bachelor pad, catching a little buzz and being completely satisfied. But being the person I am, that satisfaction didn't last long. After a couple weeks of this routine, I started looking for something more. This was the point where my life went from fairly good to bad then quickly progressed from bad to much worse.

At this point, I was thirty years old. I had recently graduated college, started working for a general contractor in Manhattan, and was living by myself in a little studio apartment in Queens. Not too bad. But for me at that time, it was not enough. I want to write down and explain exactly what happened here. I want to put my mistakes on paper for you, the reader, so you can learn from my mistakes and not have to go through the same pain and torture I put myself through.

Why wasn't I content with my life up until this point? How did I not see that I had been given the precious gift of sobriety? Why was I so eager to throw away years of hard work that earned me the career that I dreamed of? The thing is, I thought I could have both. I thought I could work during the day and party at night with minimal negative consequences. I thought I handle a little alcohol buzz and a couple lines of cocaine after work. Maybe a little heroin on the weekends.

I was able to manage my life as a night-and-weekend warrior for a little while, but it did not last long. I only wanted to spend a little bit of money, but I ended up spending all of it. I only wanted to do heroin on the weekends, but I ended up needing to do it every morning I woke up just to make it through the workday.

The first general contracting company I worked for was a small firm, but still, it was a busy company. On the day of my interview, I was instructed to speak with the head of estimating, Melissa. I was immediately impressed because I could tell she was a few years younger than me. Here I was on my first day getting into the management of construction at thirty, and I was interviewing with the head of the estimating department who was a woman in her midtwenties. I felt like I had been wasting my life for the past ten years. And on top of that, she was beautiful.

Now intimidated, I had to explain what I had been doing with my life since high school to my potential and very attractive boss. Fortunately, I was able to tell my story by only including the good things and leaving out the bad. Fast-forwarding to later in the day, I received a call letting me know I got the job and that they wanted me to start Monday. From that day on, I had a crush on Melissa. And this was at the time I was still living with Mary in Roslyn. Getting this job in Manhattan motivated me to quit working for Eddy as a carpenter. It also motivated me to leave Mary and that awful relationship and get a place of my own and pursue Melissa. And this is exactly the point in my life where I took it all for granted.

I look back at my life during this time, and I beat myself up constantly over it. What would my life be like today if I had just done the right thing and stayed sober from this point on? Also, remember, I was a few months out of rehab and living the gift of first-time sobriety. Yes, I dabbled here and there with some pills and drank occasionally, but my body and mind had not been taken over by the addiction yet. At this point, I was able to stop using when I wanted to stop using. That's part of the trick that drugs play on you. They make you believe that you are in control, at first. Then one day, you're not. And your life is never the same after that.

I'm not going to go into all the gruesome details of my drug and alcohol abuse. That's not why I'm writing. I'm writing because I want to help anyone struggling with similar issues in their lives. I want to detail what was going through my mind before I made the choices that brought about terrible negative consequences in my life. I want to detail how I maintain a sober life today and how I plan for a successful future. Your future is determined by the choices you make today. So let me summarize the next five years of my life.

I went through three more general contracting firms because once they caught on to what I was up to, they let me go at the first chance they could get. I started a relationship with Melissa and moved in with her. Eventually, my drug use tore us apart. I became resentful of everything and everyone. I left Melissa because I knew my addictions were taking over me and I didn't want her to see me at my worst. Plus, I knew I couldn't be the man I knew she deserved. I got my own apartment again in Flatbush, Brooklyn.

Are you seeing my life choice patterns here? In the Brooklyn apartment, my addiction was really spinning out of control because I invited all the drug dealers I knew inside. I wanted them as close as possible to me. I was in a very contradicting environment. I wanted to be successful in my career, but I couldn't stop using heroin. I was beginning to realize that I couldn't keep up with this lifestyle. I needed a way out of this. I was desperate for help, and I had no one to turn to. What was I supposed to do?

CHAPTER 14

THE STRUGGLE TO GET SOBER, AGAIN

It wasn't long before I found all the local drug dealers in the Brooklyn neighborhood. I was bringing home $1,200 a week, and I barely had enough money to eat. I was spending every dollar I could on drugs. I was going to work high, and everyone knew it. I think I lasted six months before I was fired. Right at the same time my project ended, so did my time at the company. I started talking to Melissa again because I honestly missed her in my life. The timing worked out to both of our advantages because her lease on her apartment was ending and she needed a place to go, and I was out of a job and couldn't pay the rent that month. Now I had to make an important decision: get sober, turn my life around, and keep Melissa in my life or continue on this reckless path of destruction, lose Melissa again, then end up in jail or dead.

The choice to get sober was easy, but the work was near impossible. And the opposite was true for my demise: the choice would be difficult, but the work is easy to stay high. I was fed up with taking the easy route. I'd been choosing the easy route for too many years, and it only made my life worse. I had so many dreams and goals I wanted to achieve, and I knew I'd never reach them if I was high on heroin. That observation had become very clear to me, and I was ready to make a drastic change in my life.

But now I was unemployed and struggling to find a new job. I was making phone calls to every GC company I could find in Manhattan. I sent in my résumé and never received a response back. This situation became scary very quickly because I had a terrible habit and still had a lot of bills to pay. It was obvious I had to give AA another serious try because I did not have the insurance or the time to admit myself into inpatient again. I needed to get my shit together quickly because rent was due in a couple weeks, and I couldn't expect Melissa to pay rent all by herself. So I started going to meetings within walking distance of my apartment two to three times a day. I had plenty of time to do this now.

As luck would have it, after weeks of following up with the emails I was sending out, I finally got a call back to come in for an interview for a well-known general contracting company. I couldn't show up to the interview high and expect everything to go well. I knew I had to clean up or I would have to go back to swinging a hammer, or worse. It was time for me to get my shit together. Not for a couple of months but for good.

With the help of Suboxone, I was able to stay away from heroin. It's a sublingual film that makes the brain think it's getting opiates, which then subsides the withdrawal effects. I was able to find someone through the internet who I could go to regularly, so I never ran out. I met my sponsor the first time I decided to go to a meeting in Manhattan. I walked up the narrow staircase above a theater playhouse that led to a second-floor apartment that was converted into an AA meeting space. I was a few minutes late because I had trouble finding the place, so the meeting had just started. And there he was, speaking to a small audience that hung on his every word. And I was one of them.

Mike took us through his life from childhood up until that day. Our lives are not identical, but they are very similar. I related to him on every level. We had not even met yet, but I felt like he understood me and I understood him. I remember thinking to myself, *If he can do it, so can I.* I was determined to get his number. I had so many questions. I was starving for wisdom, and I needed a guide in my life. I patiently waited for the meeting to end and for most of the people to leave the space before I approached him. I don't remember exactly what I said, but I know I asked for his phone number. He said, "Yeah, of course. Meet me outside." And that's where we had our first conversation. On the sidewalk of West 46th Street, outside of that theater playhouse. I'll never forget it.

We spoke for a few minutes, I gave him the story of my life summed up in a couple sentences, and he gave me my first homework assignment. We exchanged numbers that day and have kept in touch ever since. He walked me through each of the Twelve Steps and explained all the work needed to be done on my part to move on to the next step. We take our time on each step, on average completing one step per month.

By this point in my life, I had had enough of the torture and suffering that the drugs were causing in my life. I was now determined to get sober and stay sober. I was ready to continue a serious relationship with Melissa. I was about to start working for a new company. I wanted to regain the confidence and trust of my parents. I wanted to improve my life only and stop destroying it. I was going to AA meetings regularly and participating. I was keeping in touch with my sponsor and working on the steps. I was doing everything I was supposed to do, and still I was struggling to find peace in my body and mind.

I still forgot that I had been under the influence for about fifteen years. Just because I was done with the drugs that didn't mean the drugs were not done with me. My body was still highly addicted, and I could hear it constantly reminding me of that. There was no time to waste. I was so desperate to be rid this life-taking addiction. I didn't have time to find a doctor because I didn't have insurance at the time, so with the help of Craigslist, I was able to get Suboxone on the street.

If you are familiar with Craigslist, you know that the majority of the ads on there are bullshit and you do not want to waste your time with the people advertising on there. Luckily, after much trial and error, I found someone that answered the phone and who sounded like a normal enough person to meet up with. I had to travel about an hour uptown into the Bronx, to an area I had never been before, but it was worth the risk. I got enough medication to last me a couple weeks, made a new friend, then headed back home.

You would think I'm in the clear now, right? All I had to do was take the Suboxone as prescribed and I'd be fine. Yes and no. There is invisible print that is marked on every sublingual strip of Suboxone. And that is "Before you ingest this, you must be free of heroin for twenty-four hours. If taken before twenty-four hours of your last use, this medication will send you violently into withdrawal." In all honesty, I was using heroin about once every eight hours. Now I had to wait a full twenty-four hours before taking this medication.

On the first day, I had some confidence that I could stick it out. I stayed busy during the day going to meetings and cleaning around the apartment to pass the time. I was a little shaky but not completely insane yet. The time to go to bed had arrived, and I was anxious to start a new day and a fresh sober journey. Sometime around one a.m., I woke up in a sweat. Panic started to set in. I went to the bathroom to pee, and pretended everything was fine. I laid back down in bed and closed my eyes, took a few deep breaths, and allowed myself to drift back into dreamland.

About twenty seconds later, it hit me again. I squeezed my eyes down tight, flipped the pillow, and rolled over to my other side. Ten seconds later, I was hit again. Now my eyes were wide-open, and I was beginning to realize that withdrawal was upon me. Instead of tossing and turning in our bed, I got up again to go lie on the couch. I didn't want to wake up Melissa or let her know how much I was struggling.

Now I was on the living room couch with my pillow and a thin blanket. The moonlight seeped in through the slats of the window shades. I was surrounded by pale moonlight, panic, and the onset of heroin withdrawal. I could no longer lie down. From this point on, finding comfort was out of the question. I was sitting up on the couch with a blanket over my back, clutching my pillow in my lap, and violently rocking back and forth. My skin was burning up. It felt like fiberglass was running through my veins. Noxiousness would not leave my intestines; I was dry heaving every few minutes. Then

I was bombarded by cold flashes. Now I was biting my pillow hard enough to break my teeth.

I looked for the time. My mouth had become as dry as the desert, and my heart sank into my stomach when I read that it was only 1:15 a.m. Those fifteen minutes just felt like fifteen hours. I had to do this until seven a.m.? As I rocked back and forth on the couch, I contemplated calling my drug dealer so I could make this torture go away. Then I remembered the promise I made to myself to get sober. I constantly reminded myself, *I will get through this. I can do this. I can do this. God, please help me get through this. I can get through this. I can do this.*

Again, I checked the time: 1:30 a.m. I practiced my mantra over and over and over as I rocked back and forth on that sweaty couch. I got through an hour. Then another hour. As time went on, my panic increased. My sanity diminished. The screams in my head got louder and louder. *Make this go away!* Tears were running down my face. Giving up and giving in seemed to be the only thing that made sense in this moment. I pulled my drug dealer's contact up on my phone and stared it at. I knew that by pressing the Call button, I was officially giving up on my freedom. I would be breaking the promise I made to myself. At the same time, my brain felt like it was three times larger and about to break through my skull.

I had to give in. I couldn't keep this up. Thoughts of suicide were appearing in my mind, and I refused to entertain those thoughts. After a long stare at the phone number, I pressed Call. I made the arrangements and bolted out onto the street at 3:30 a.m. I barely had $10. Just enough for one bag. But that was enough. That was enough to silence my mind to where I could get some sleep. I promised myself again, *I'm going to get sober, tomorrow.*

This routine lasted about two weeks. Every day I woke up with confidence that I would make it twenty-four hours without using so I could safely get onto the opioid medication. And every night I broke another promise to myself to avoid going completely insane. I was making progress though. Each night I lasted a little longer before giving up. I could not believe the joy I felt when I realized, finally, I had made it through the torture of withdrawal long enough to open the package of Suboxone.

After about five minutes of the medication being placed under my tongue, I felt my withdrawal begin to melt away. I was so happy I cried. After years of torture and suffering, all I wanted was relief. Relief from the constant demands of my addictions. And then finally, as relief sets in, withdrawal symptoms fade away and a new feeling begins to form. Something that I had not felt in a very long while… faith.

CHAPTER 15

WATCH YOURSELF
FROM A DISTANCE

We're made to believe, all our lives, that we will become anything we want in life: cowboy, ninja, famous artist, professional football or basketball player, movie star, rock star. Those were my career choices as a kid. Once I reached my twenties, I realized these dreams of mine were more likely to remain dreams rather than becoming my reality.

During eleventh grade, I was pressured to pick a college major. None of my original choices were an option for me, and that's when reality hit me hard. That's when I began to settle for second best and mediocrity. I have been cursed with an "all or nothing" personality. Once I have to settle for second best, I begin to lose my enthusiasm in what I am doing and for my life itself. Straight out of high school, I enrolled in college. I first studied architecture because I appreciated the talent it takes to build a house. But I was involved in something that was not my first choice, so I had a very difficult time being interested. I was living a reality that felt like someone else had chosen it for me. So the option of escaping my reality started looking really good.

Drinking malt liquor and smoking weed before and after class became a habit and a welcomed new lifestyle. And again, my "all or nothing" personality took control of something it felt like it had control over. This was my ego at work. My ego thought it was helping me by getting high before class so that class wouldn't seem so bad, so my life wouldn't be so sad and boring. I was still a teenager then, and I didn't even know what my ego was. I was being led around by my impulses and my lack of patience. From here, I lost control of my life more and more. I consistently made reckless choice after reckless choice. The more I escaped my reality, the more it haunted me. I was unconsciously making my life worse and worse, becoming less and less in control of my choices and actions. That is how I, unconsciously, created a very difficult life for myself.

Let's talk about healing on the emotional and spiritual level. Let's talk about ways to find relief from our inner suffering. That's what this book is all about. It's about experiencing true healing and finding relief from suffering. The first thing that must be realized is that you are loved just the way you are. You do not have to change anything about yourself to be accepted and loved. Love cannot be taken or stolen. Love is earned. Do not "think" about the right thing to say. Allow the next right thing to flow through you. Wait for it to come to you. Allow yourself to be a conduit through which the universe flows. There is nothing to practice here. You are already connected to the universe and can access its energy at any time.

All that is required is your realization of this truth. Realize your connection with the universe (God). Realize the universe loves you just the way you are. Realize that you have great potential to make your dreams a reality. Give yourself permission to love and respect yourself. Give yourself permission to be happy and content with yourself and the progress you have made. Realize that perfection is only a direction and not a destination. Realize that to improve your quality of life, you must practice and work toward reaching your goals.

One of my biggest weaknesses is having little to no patience. I want to own a home now. But in reality, even though I work my ass off and save my money, it will still take a long time for me to save enough money to own a home. I still struggle with having patience, but I know that if I keep doing what I'm doing, eventually, I will get to where I'm trying to go. Also, I want to be really good at playing the guitar. As of now, I am a beginner. But if I practice, the right way, I will eventually get better and better.

You can apply that formula to pretty much anything in life. Luck can sometimes play a role and catapult you toward success, but you must put yourself in a position to receive such luck. In other words, surround yourself with people that are more advanced than you. If possible, way more advanced than you. The gravitational pull of their success will more likely than not affect you too.

Let's talk about sexual orientation and identity. It is no one's business who you love but your own. I believe everyone loves someone. What matters is the love. Regarding your family and friends approving your relationship, their number one concern should be your happiness. Does this person make you happy? If yes, everything will naturally fall into place. This should not be a political topic.

Identity can be more of an extensive topic because each person in the world has their own unique qualities. I believe love is a more universal feeling, emotion, and expression. For the most part, we all describe love with a very similar definition. When you ask about identity, you will get a different definition from each person. There will be similarities and connections made when calling out identities, and that is what I'm interested in: similarities and connections. What makes us human? Where did humans come from? What is the content of the energy that causes us to be alive? What is the energy within us that causes us to live and breathe? Where did it come from? How does it replenish and maintain itself? Where does it go when our bodies die?

What is important to you? Why is it important? The most important spiritual lesson that I have learned and still practice is "You are not your thoughts." You are not your body. You are not your emotions. You are not your mind. Do not give your thoughts much significance. Your mind produces thoughts just like your heart beats and pumps blood. These organs are important, without a doubt, but they should not rule your life or your existence.

You are your awareness. You are your consciousness. That is the real you. The real you is your spirit, your soul. These are all synonyms when speaking spiritually. We inherited the same consciousness of the suns, moons, and planets. We inherited the consciousness of the universe. Why would you limit yourself only to your thoughts and emotions? Here's a common question or response to this: "How do I do that? How do I become one with the universe? How do I allow the universe to flow through me?"

First, consider these words to be true. You have to be willing to accept this as your true spiritual identity. If you think or feel this is all bullshit, then this will not work for you. Being open to new possibilities, I believe, is the foundation for all human growth on every level. Then practice witnessing your thoughts and emotions without judging or labeling them in any way. Practice nonjudgment to everything being experienced through your five senses. Become in tune with all five of your senses because those five senses are the thin line between what is you and what is not you.

Begin to realize that for us to stay alive, we must be in constant contact with the five elements of planet Earth. We need the earth, and the earth needs us. We need the universe just as the universe needs us. The universe wants us to recognize it. The universe wants us to be aware of its existence. The universe becomes conscious of itself through us. We breathe what the trees exhale, and the trees breathe what we exhale. That is just one example.

While witnessing your thoughts arise then fade away, begin to create a space within you, begin to recognize the space between your awareness and your thoughts. Although these thoughts belong to us, they are not you. The real you is much more vast than a thought. The real you is the vast space that allows the thoughts to exist. Just witness, just internally watch as your thoughts arise then fade away. Then a new thought arises then fades away. Again and again. Play close attention to space in between the thoughts—the few milliseconds of the empty space from where the previous thought faded away to right before a new thought arises. That space of silence and stillness, that is the real you. The vast space of infinity. The divine. The space where infinite potential lives. That is the real you.

It has always been there and always will be there. It is up to you how much you tap into that infinite energy field. The amazing thing is that you only need to recognize this for a few seconds to feel the power within you. This is one fluid motion, one step. A wise spiritual being does not need to know many things. Only one thing: that he/she is neither the body nor the mind.

Here's an example to think about. Ask yourself this question: Which one is the real you? You as a baby? You as a child? You as a teenager? You as an adult? Or the form you are now in? Which form or version is the real you? Isn't it true that we are constantly changing? Isn't it true that we are constantly evolving? Compare your thoughts and view on the world from when you were a child to that of when you were a teenager. Compare your thoughts and views on the world from when you were a teenager to how you see the world, and yourself, now. Our bodies are constantly changing and evolving. Our minds are constantly changing and evolving. What has been the one constant? Your soul. Otherwise known as your awareness, your consciousness.

As a teenager and in my twenties, I was moved by an inner drum to celebrate and party. Now in my thirties, I'm moved by a similar inner drumbeat. But the focus is to advance in my career and provide for my family. My interests have changed. My priorities have changed. And it feels like the right thing to do within every cell of my being.

When speaking spiritually, I define responsibility as how I respond to my environment: an emotionally mature response, a responsible response. Your ability to respond to your environment is infinite. I bring this up because sometimes I find myself not wanting to be bothered by anyone or anything. Sometimes I just want to be left alone. And that's okay, but not when you are responsible for being present for someone. For instance, if it is time to go food shopping and my wife asks me to go with her to help carry the groceries, I am responsible to say yes. Even though I'm in the middle of a movie or it will be inconveniencing my Sunday plans to just chill out.

I am responsible to accept and go with the flow of my environment. If I were to say no and reject the flow of my environment, I will only be making my life more difficult as this would be like swimming against the current. My Sunday would be much less chill. Even if my wife didn't mind that I stay home, I wouldn't be able to fully enjoy my time to myself because I would be haunted by my own guilt of not being a man when a man is called for. In reality, I can pause whatever I was doing to be there for someone other than myself. Then I can return to my work or chill zone afterward. That would be responsibly responding to my environment. If someone asks for directions, it starts to snow outside, a longtime friend is calling you, you have fifty unread emails at work…you have an infinite ability to responsibly respond to them all. One at a time. Without any frustration.

Life is what we make it. Every situation we are in is a direct consequence of a previous decision we have made. What kind of a life have I created for myself? What kind of a life will I create for my kids? Will I be able to control my anger when my patience wears thin? Will I have the energy to spend time with them and raise them right? Will I be able to determine when to apply life lessons and when to just go with the flow? Will I have enough money to take care of them? I will try to do my best. But I feel I should start preparing for it now. My kids are already being formed through my awareness and my thoughts. They will be a product of love. I am looking forward to creating life and then to teaching them how to live. I will be teaching them how to live while at the same time still finding answers to my own life questions.

I am starting to see that my maturity is developing further as I get older. I am able to recognize when my childlike ego starts to take over and begins to complain about my current situations. A lot of times it starts with not wanting to be where I am at any given time. The morning is especially difficult for me. I awake from dreamland, and I am immediately placed in reality. There's a part of me that wants to go back to dreamland and not have to face my reality. But my life isn't really that bad anymore. That's what I'm starting to realize.

I have everything I need. Maybe not everything I want, but I definitely have what I need. I have made a lot of progress in my life. Not as much as I wish I would have by now, but still. I have come a long way. I feel like I'm still growing. I say that because for the past year or so, I've been dealing with consistent back pain right in the middle of my spine. Is my spine getting longer? I'm not sure. But maybe it is. Why would that be impossible? I definitely have what I need to keep moving forward in life and start to enjoy every step of the way instead of dreading it.

Sometimes I wish I could fast-forward to when I'm fifty years old and well established. I want to fast-forward to where my kids are grown, my investments are steadily growing, and I'm getting ready to retire from my management career. I want to own a five-story apartment building and live off the rent coming in every month. I would have more time to paint my abstract artwork and more time to be a helping hand in the community, especially within AA. I want to be healthy and wealthy so I can take care of myself, my family, and the people around me. That sounds like a complete life to me. I feel myself getting a little closer every day.

I feel I don't have much to offer now because I'm still trying to get my shit together. But I have a well-thought-out plan for my future. I'm really starting to see how a bright future could be possible for me. A big weakness I have is spending my money on crap I don't need. That has to stop if I'm going to be able to save any substantial amount of money. There are always going to be more things that I want to have. Majority of these things are not necessary to my survival. They only seem to be necessary to my self-worth, according to my ego. If I look good, then I feel good. But there is a limit to that.

I have run out of room for more tattoos. I have run out of room in my closet for more clothes. There is no more space in my apartment for anymore gadgets. I have given away good stuff just so I can replace it with new stuff. In the end, it's all just stuff that takes up room and turns into clutter. I need more self-discipline and control over my impulses.

I can remember a time in my life when I had all the discipline a seventh grader could possibly have. At that time, I was very determined to get into a good college with the hopes of being drafted into the NBA or the NFL. My plan B was to become an artist working as a cartoonist for TV and movies. I kept this dream alive for a while. I was working out just about every day. I was getting all As in school.

My parents were happy with me, but I had no friends. I became completely introverted. I spent most of my time alone working out, studying, drawing, and practicing my basketball skills out in the street.

My dad put up a basketball hoop on the sidewalk, and I was out there constantly working on my dribbling and my jump shot. I was second string on the JV football team. I had high hopes that if I practiced enough, I would get my shot as a starting wide receiver. I really practiced hard. I took it all very seriously—so serious that if I was anything short of perfection, I would get very disappointed in myself and become very frustrated. I would scream through my teeth if I didn't make three perfect jump shots in a row. I cursed myself if I ever dropped a pass from the quarterback or from anyone. What happened to that dream? To those beliefs? I think they started to fade when I was cut from the varsity basketball team. This was when I got my first taste of despair. The discipline I had for keeping myself healthy was declining quickly. I was drinking more often and seeking escape through drug use.

In my twenties, I found myself never wanting to be where I was. I wanted to escape my own existence and surroundings. It was rare for me to be comfortable in my own skin and content with where I was at that current moment. I've been disappointed in myself with my financial status because I always knew I should have been saving my money instead of always spending all of it. The past twenty years of my life has been so wasteful on so many levels. My happiness and contentment began with me being okay with where I am regarding all aspects. It's an inner acceptance. I have learned that my life unfolds as a series of choices, one after the next. Each of those choices has a consequence, whether it be good or bad.

I create my reality. I have come to believe that I alone create my current experience. I create it by how I am perceiving it through my awareness, through judgments, opinions, and critique of what's happening in front of me. Based on what has happened to me in my past, I create judgments and decisions on what to do at the current moment or how to feel about the situation unfolding in front of me.

I decide what matters, and by giving the important matter my attention, the matter becomes alive.

I have learned something very important during my sober journey. Every morning, I thank God for returning me to sanity. I thank God for my health. Every morning I gently ask, "God, please grant me the strength to get through this day. Please grant me the courage and wisdom to get through this day. Please help me gain financial security so that I may become a great provider for my family." This prayer of mine is my daily maintenance. It either brings me up or down to size, depending on how my life is going at that time. It is my way of staying in contact with the universe. I've noticed that if I do nothing, my brain reverts back to the old habits very quickly. It is not long before I am wallowing in self-pity and asking myself, "How did I get here again?"

I have gone from hating myself to respecting myself. Faith in a brighter future has appeared within me for the first time in a very long time, and I am beginning to believe in myself again. My perspective has gone from "I guess I have to keep doing this" to "I get to do this." To me, that's a very big and important change in perspective. With everything else in my life, my progress is slow. It always seems to start with small slow steps toward my goal. Then after a little while, I begin to accelerate and become able to take much wider strides.

I can come up with many reasons why I started using drugs. But after all the education and rehabs and AA meetings, it's hard to say why I continued to use. Escaping reality is definitely one reason. But the main reason is very difficult for me to admit to myself or to anyone. I'm an addict. I have developed an addiction to a few bad things and have altered the chemicals and pathways in my brain. I never used to describe myself as or identified with being an addict. It was always a sore spot for me. I don't want to call myself an addict. I don't want other people to know me as an addict. But in reality, I am. I have all the characteristics and tendencies of an addict.

But I did not experience true sobriety until I was actually able to admit to myself that I am an addict. Once I began to accept my weaknesses as being a part of my identity, I was able to live my life without hiding. That was when I truly started to feel freedom from my addictions. I have accepted what I cannot do. This makes it more clear what I can do. The opposite of rejection, acceptance, is how I regained my positive outlook on life. Through my acceptance of life, the elusive seed of confidence can grow.

CHAPTER 16

HOW DO I GET OVER MY HEARTBREAK?

Good question, right? I have asked many people how to get over my trauma and heartbreak. The most common answer I get is "Start over with someone new." I agree that this will help, but I don't believe the pain will completely go away just because a new friend or a new love has entered your life. Although, there is a possibility that a new relationship could help you find relief from your pain. But let's start at the beginning, with the pain. I will speak from my own experience because these perspectives have helped me accept and let go.

I've been hurt emotionally many times. Before I knew what heartbreak was, I would allow myself to become completely obsessed with the one I lusted after. That's how it was for me. I saw a girl that I was attracted to then I worked my way over to her so I could introduce myself and learn her name. Sometimes, it went well. And sometimes I tried too hard and would scare her away. Either way, for a couple of the relationships that went well at first, I allowed myself to become head-over-heels, head-in-the-clouds obsessed in love.

Then when she broke up with me, I fell hard. My heart felt like it literally exploded inside my chest and that it was no longer there. The depression I felt was a constant sinking feeling from within. I became hollow. My personality was gone. My emotions were gone. I was floating through life as an empty shell of a person. I stopped caring about everything and everyone, including myself. That's when my drinking and drug use was shifted into overdrive. And I have learned the hard way that self-destruction is not the answer!

Forgiveness is the answer. As difficult as it is, close your eyes and picture the one that hurt you. Use a pleasant memory of when you were both together. Put yourself back at that moment and say, "I forgive you." This next step is even more painful, but you must power through it. Pray for their happiness. Something like "God, please let them find happiness today." At first, you probably won't mean it. But after some time, you might surprise yourself to find you really did mean that last one. Through honest forgiveness, we can find acceptance. And through acceptance, you can let go.

Now, on to you. Are you mad at yourself for doing something stupid? Look yourself in the mirror and say, "I forgive you." Don't you wish you could go back in time as the wise person you are now and warn the younger, much more naive, you? Let's do that now. Close your eyes and picture yourself as a young teenager. With your eyes still closed, kneel down on one knee. Look directly at younger you and say something along the lines of "Listen up, smart-ass, because I'm probably only going to do this once. I know you have a lot of big dreams and beautiful hopes for the future, but the world is not as magical as you think it is. You're not going to be able to make friends with everyone. There are some people that will only take advantage of your kindness and leave you with nothing. You will only need one hand to count all your true friends. So please, do not give away your trust so easily. Don't be so impulsive. Go slow and take your time when making important decisions. I forgive you for not seeing what lies ahead. But still, never give up on your dreams. Never give up on yourself. And for God's sake, be patient. Anything worth having takes hard work and a long time to get it. Now get out there and kick some ass!"

What do you think younger you would say to you now? Younger me would lower his eyebrows, take a deep breath, and say, "Stop feeling sorry for yourself. How could you forget how amazing you are? Stop eating that crap and get your ass back in the gym. I didn't give up. You gave up. Your talent didn't leave. You just stopped practicing. Who cares what other people think? I know you can be great at what you do, did you forget? What makes you think you can't do it? Because some asshole said so. Fuck that! Move on. Ignore them and keep going. Only jealous people say that shit. Regain your confidence in yourself. I forgive you for losing your sense of wonder, but stand up straight and get your shit together. You have the heart of a lion. Now get out there and kick some ass!"

I understand that this might sound crazy as a way to get over heartbreak, but it won't hurt you to try this. You don't have to kneel down when you do this; you could just envision the whole thing. I'm trying to provide a template for bridging the gap between all the different versions of yourself. From young to teenager to midtwenties to the current you. Even though each version is slightly different, they are all one and the same. They all share the same unchanging soul.

Every step you have made, every decision you have made, has led you to this moment. This is also related to your karma. Begin to realize that you have the ability to shape your future through the decisions that you make. Start making conscious decisions to let go of the past and begin to see a very possible brighter future for yourself. If you're like me, you might be telling yourself that you don't deserve to be happy subconsciously. Recognize this and stop allowing it to happen. Tell yourself that you do deserve to be happy. Because you do. Tell yourself that you do deserve to be loved. Because you do.

CHAPTER 17

WE ARE ADDICTED TO OUR OWN LIMITATIONS

Some limitations are self-created. The only thing stopping me from writing a book was me telling myself I couldn't do it. I told myself I didn't have the time. I convinced myself that I had nothing important or interesting to say. Then a few years ago, I started transferring my notes that I had written in notebooks into a Word document. Little by little, I added new topics that came to me when they came to me. The total number of pages started to increase slowly, but it was progress nonetheless. Chapter topics started to form. Then I was able to edit it in such a way where the book read as a continuous thought as opposed to scattered, random thoughts.

Now there is only one challenge to work through and that is to continue. To finish what I started. This involves having patience with myself and my progress. Of course, I wish I could just fast-forward in time to a place where the book is complete, but then I would be missing the great satisfaction that comes with reaching a long-term goal. I face that dilemma every time I open the laptop. But I need to work through this, from the beginning to the end. I have to see this through. I have put something in motion, and honestly, it's easier for me to continue writing and editing than it would be if I were to stop halfway through and give up. I would be filled with so much regret that I gave up willingly. My dreams would turn into nightmares. My reality would be dreadful and apocalyptic instead of hopeful and confident.

This formula applies to everything I do in life. I must believe in myself and take the calculated risks toward reaching my goals. If I choose not to work toward my goals, I'm essentially choosing death over life. I would be allowing the wind to take me wherever it throws me. Instead, I consciously take each step forward knowing that each step I take is one more step closer to reaching that goal. There are some things that we have no control over, but there are some things that we do. We must learn the difference between the two, and we usually learn that lesson as we go.

Human beings have an amazing ability to adapt to their environment. I have found that the most difficult thing to overcome, on the subconscious level, is my own insecurities and a disbelief in myself. The inner forces within ourselves (controllable) seem to be stronger than the outer forces (uncontrollable). What do you think would happen if you stopped allowing yourself from holding you back?

CHAPTER 18

JESUS HAS NO RACE

As a kid, life seemed so magical. I remember being filled with wonder. Do you remember that? I'm talking about being eight or nine years old. I don't remember ever feeling pain or feeling cold. I remember genuinely looking forward to holidays and birthdays. I loved hanging out with neighborhood friends and playing with my action figures, playing outside during the summer with Super Soakers and running through lawn sprinklers, playing outside in the winter snow and building igloos and snowmen, playing outside in the fall and diving into a big pile of leaves. What happened to that? Does it go away just because we grow up and our interests change? I understand that at some point we have to put our childish toys down and grow up, but does that mean our sense of wonder and imagination go with them too?

For me, I think I started to lose my magical view of the world when I was told that Santa was not real. I'm the oldest of four. I have two sisters and one brother. So I had to pretend Santa was real for them for a few additional years. As we grow up, we are taught that Santa is watching us and makes a list of the nice kids and bad kids. Nice kids get presents and bad kids get coal. We're being taught to behave with the incentive of receiving toys. When we get older, our incentive is getting into heaven when we die. Or going to hell because of our sins. As children we are told that Santa magically watches us somehow. Or he has helpers such as little elves or birds that go back and tell him how we're doing.

If you can believe this at a young age, then the idea of our grandparents watching us from heaven isn't a far stretch. Our parents are our gods when we are children. We rely on them for everything. We trust and believe them when they ask us to leave out some cookies and milk for Santa. It's like a peace offering, and we do it. We set up the cookies and milk right near where you want him to drop off all those presents. If your parents are going all in with the Santa thing, they will leave a couple half-eaten cookies left on the plate. As a kid, I really believed Santa visited our house dropping off presents, filling the stockings, eating cookies and milk, then going on to the next good boys and girls.

You know, it's not really year 2020. It's more like fourteen million and 2020. Our year is set to the birth of Jesus. Every time we celebrate a new year, we are celebrating another year into Jesus's life even after his death. We are celebrating Jesus's life without even realizing it.

The wilderness of the forest is a peaceful place. So is the beach, near crashing waves. Wandering in the wilderness is symbolism of where spirituality crystalizes. It's a place for reflection and retrospection. This is where Jesus meets the devil in the Bible. Jesus considers but does not give into the devil's temptations.

We have to explore the limits of the law and of the rules. That's the best way to understand them and to know them well. This is a normal part of the Jewish religion. They are trained to question the Torah as a way to know the religion better. Rebellion is essential to maturity. The Bible says that Jesus was baptized by John the Baptist, a known rebellious preacher, in the River Jordan. Baptism means eternal life. Without John the Baptist, we may have never had Jesus as we know him. Jesus is known for performing miracles like giving sight to the blind. I feel this is a metaphor in the Bible for the man that was not literally blind. The blind man was likely a thief. He was blind in the sense that he could not clearly see the peaceful ways of the Christian religion.

Did Jesus really walk on water, or did he swim across that lake? Did Jesus really turn water into wine, or did he learn how to ferment grapes? Food and wine were ultimate treasures in Jesus's lifetime because there was never enough of it. Jesus teaches us how to live our lives with concern for others. He teaches good behavior, ethics, and responsibility within the family and community. Jesus had a commanding presence. He was a charismatic speaker and storyteller. People left their families and homes to follow him. John the Baptist and Jesus preached the end of the world and the apocalypse. They urged their followers to repent and to change their self-serving ways now before it was too late.

Jesus said, "Blessed are the meek, for they shall inherit the earth." *Meek* does not mean weak or feeble. *Meek* means the people who live simply and practically. Peaceful and forgiving people. People who value life over material possessions. Jesus walked through towns and villages with men and women followers. The women were older and from well-off means. They were most likely the ones funding his travels as they spread his message within the homes of other women.

Mary Magdalene was known to be the sinner who turned saint. She washed Jesus's feet with water and dried them with her hair. Since she was one of Jesus's followers, other women wanted to be like her. Because Mary Magdalene was popular and admired by the other Catholic women, a certain pope spread a rumor that she was a prostitute. The reason being so that the other women wouldn't try to get a lofty place in the church right next to Jesus.

Jesus first preached in the north. Then with a big following, he headed south to Jerusalem during Passover. On these travels, he brought Lazarus back from the dead. Jesus said, "I am the resurrection and the life and whoever believes in me shall never die." I will interpret this as "The spirit is eternal.: Jesus only lasted a few days in Jerusalem before he was arrested. The Jews had been waiting for a messiah to rescue them from the oppression of the Romans, but they did not see him as their messiah. Jesus went from Galilee to Jerusalem preaching a radical apocalyptic message. We find out that Jesus was betrayed by one of his followers, Judas. He was bribed with some silver by the authorities to point out the one who claimed to be the son of God.

Once arrested, Jesus welcomed his showdown with the high priest. The religion of the time did, in fact, teach that all human beings are children of God. But Jesus was claiming he was divine. The Pharisees took pride in their lineage by boasting that they were sons of Abraham. Jesus was challenging the Pharisees, telling them that they were no better than the burning bodies of the poor. So he was handed over to the Romans to be killed. Pontius Pilate saw Jesus as a threat because Jesus was called the King of the Jews by his followers. Pontius Pilate had Jesus whipped and given a crown of thorns. Some Bible scriptures say that Pilate gave the watching audience a choice to save Jesus or to save another man who was on trial. The crowd condemned Jesus, so Pilate ordered him to be crucified. After Jesus's death, he is resurrected and brought up to heaven, making him a divine being and also making his death not the end of his life.

Jesus's race is a mystery. It is supposed to be a mystery. Jesus's race is not what is significant to his teachings. What matters is his message. I believe Jesus was a real man. I believe that the Bible was written by his closest followers with the intention of documenting his life and putting his teachings on paper because they are both so profound. The Bible was not originally written in English and has been translated many times over. Just like the game of Telephone, some of the stories and some of the meaning gets lost in translation. Some events may have been deleted, added, or embellished. When reading about Buddha, Muhammed, and Jesus, I notice a similarity. They were all real people who actually existed. They came to believe in a power much greater than themselves, and they lived selflessly. It seems their sole purpose is to pass along their message of peace, love, and understanding. Everything they do is for the greater good of mankind.

I have come to believe that most religions are all very similar. The only major difference is the name of the leader. To me, they are all the same amazing person. The only reason why I consider myself Catholic is because that's what was taught to me and practiced when I was growing up.

How do you see this world and your surroundings? Because I believe you get what you give. Do you see the world as an amazingly beautiful place and in a perfect, delicate balance? Not enough people talk about how to live. I think most people hesitate because of fear of negative criticism. But there are too many people looking for answers not to talk about it. A popular saying is "Be the change you want to see in the world, and people will follow." So why do we do the wrong thing even though we know what the right thing is? It's a simple question with a complicated answer.

No artist can compete with Jesus's fame. Everyone knows who Jesus was or, at the very least, has heard of him. Same goes for Buddha and Muhammed. Jesus can be considered the boss of Christianity. When he passed on to the next form, he passed down the family business to his disciples. To his next of kin. When the family business is passed down to the next generation, the foundation of ethics, integrity, public interest, and well-being that the company was built on gets lost. The new leaders of the company are mainly focused on the money, on how to expand its reach and influence on a global scale. The basic equation is "The more believers we have, the more money we make. How do we keep the believers believing in us? We will scare them into making them do what we want them to do. We will control them with fear."

Jesus's original message was all about transforming your life for the better and to find and live in heaven here on earth. Atonement and salvation. Rapture and Zion. Awakening, zen, enlightenment, communion with divinity, and salvation. Revelation and Armageddon. The beginning and the end. Genesis and the apocalypse.

Then the church turned the main message into "If you're not good, you're going to hell." The message's tone went from based in love into a message based in fear. From fear, hate and division is born. From love, unity is born. Religion and our beliefs of life and of life after death are important. Always have been and always will be. As modern, more intelligent, and more aware human beings, we must be able to find the true and pure teachings of our religions. Take what you like and leave the rest. The original teachings of all religions are

96

spiritually based. That's the wisdom we need right now in our societies throughout the world.

When we hear the word *apocalypse*, several images run through our minds: fire and flood, earthquakes and tidal waves, crumbling societies, and zombies. But when the word *apocalypse* came into the English language in the 1200s, it referred to none of these things. The word *apocalypse* was initially used to refer to a particular type of Jewish and Christian writing that was common between 200 BC and 150 AD and used symbolic imagery to foretell the end of this world and the future to come. The best-known apocalyptic work is the book of Revelation. The Greek word that gave us *apocalypse* means "to uncover or to reveal."

Jesus spoke with an apocalyptic message to reveal the truths of how people were living, to warn the people that an evil lifestyle would lead them to a future filled with chaos, destruction, and pain. Apocalyptic writings were often filled with cataclysmic events that ended the present age and caused the dawning of the age to come. These world-ending events included fires, earthquakes, and heavenly armies fighting. A few centuries after the word *apocalypse* entered the English language to name this style of literature, the word gained two additional meanings. One that referred to the final battle between good and evil and another to refer to any disaster with far-reaching and devastating effects.

The battle between good and evil is at the core of all religious teachings. Let's not debate over whether I'm getting into heaven or going to hell when I pass on. Let's figure out how to create a heavenly life here on earth instead of creating a life of hell for myself. The Bible and all religious books are supposed to make you think. Do not take the stories and fables literally or as a foretelling of the future. The intent is to make you reflect on your lifestyle and choices. Your lifestyle and choices ultimately determine your future of an existence of living in hell or an existence of living in heaven.

Hell is not a biblical staple. The original passage of the Bible never actually mentions hell. Much of the Bible is debatable and is open to numerous interpretations. The Bible has been translated many times; and the King James Bible, which is widely considered to be one of the most inaccurate translations, is also a fixture in traditional Christian circles. Hell is a modern concept of a place of eternal torment. As humans, we seem to be fantastic at creating hell for ourselves. We sow it into our own lives and the lives of our loved ones and everyone around us.

But Jesus came to bring us salvation. In his human form, he experienced the joys of life and the hellish torments of our existence. Then he introduced us to a benevolent Father, the Creator or God. He came to show us the way of life, the path to get through our personal hell; and when he left, he announced the arrival of our guide, the Holy Spirit, who would help us navigate our righteous path in life. The Holy Spirit exists within all of us and all around us.

If hell is such a central part of sin, judgment, and death and if God is actually planning on casting out billions of people, allowing them to burn for all eternity, shouldn't it be mentioned a lot more in the Bible? Is God the cruelest, most perversely genocidal maniac in history? Or are we translating the message incorrectly?

Most of the confusion around hell is due to translation error. There are four separate Hebrew and Greek words that are translated into the English word *hell*. *Sheol*—the "world of the dead," "grave," "pit." *Hades*—the "place of departed souls." *Tartarus*—to "incarcerate in eternal torment." *Gehenna*—a valley of Jerusalem, a place of perpetual burning.

The English language is often very limited when trying to express certain concepts. A perfect biblical example of this are the multiple Greek words translated to the single English word *love*. *Agape*—a special version of love that speaks about God's love toward humanity. *Phileo*—brotherly love. *Eros*—refers to sexual love or desire. And just like *love*, the English word *hell* is disjointedly translated from the Greek and Hebrew words *Sheol, Hades, Gehenna*, and *Tartarus*. Each of these have different meanings.

Gehenna is a literal valley, a physical geographic location in Israel. A section of this valley was well-known throughout Israel as an evil and dark place used by the rebellious Israelites for child sacrifice to honor their pagan gods. As time went on, people began dumping and burning their trash in this valley. Gehenna was a place of continuous fire that would constantly burn away whatever was not wanted inside the city, including dead bodies. The valley contained so much trash and dead bodies that the worms that ate them would never die from lack of sustenance.

Jesus was using the most disgusting location in Jerusalem to illustrate how destructive sin is and to encourage his followers to overcome it now so they could freely enjoy an abundant life instead of falling into self-destructive patterns. Jesus was pointing to a literal pile of burning bodies and comparing it to what your life could become if you continue a life of sin. Sin is not meaningless. It is literally inviting hell into your life.

Everything begins from your awareness. Then as it travels through your senses, you decide whether it is favorable or unfavorable through your perception. Awareness exists before your vision. Before your vision and your thoughts. Before any one of your five senses and your thoughts/emotions. But until you direct your awareness toward something, that something will not exist in your personal world. Whatever you are not aware of does not exist for you. This is how I can say that everything begins from your awareness.

Nothing matters and everything matters at the same time. I am nothing and everything at the same time. It's easy and complicated at the same time. This body is me, but it's not mine. I have to give it back at some point.

For me, my growing up had a lot to do with becoming a mature adult. I had a very difficult time battling the kid within me. The first step to not giving the immature kid in me the control is to recognize when he starts to kick and scream for what he wants. I stopped giving myself any excuses to be upset with myself. I stopped avoiding the work that needed to get done. This is the incomplete work that stands in the way of my happiness and satisfaction with myself. The easiest thing to start with is cleaning your apartment. Take everything out of the drawers and closets and bags, and throw away what is actually garbage. Make a separate pile of things you can give away to family and friends. Then reorganize your storage areas so everything is neat until your living space makes sense. And of course, vacuum and wipe everything down. It might take a few hours, but once you're all done with your cleaning and rearranging, I guarantee you will feel a little weight lift off your shoulders. Maybe even a lot.

I applied this "out with the bad and in with the good" style of work to my life as well. I stopped hanging out with the drinking buddies and fair-weather friends. I call my mom and dad more often to repair our relationship. I gained back the trust of my brother and sisters again by showing them it was possible for me to live a sober life. While at work, my focus became so much stronger now that I stopped poisoning myself. I was given more responsibility, and in turn, a slight increase in pay. Here's something I had never done before: save more money than I spent. That change in behavior was huge for me because now I could save and prepare for my future to become a provider for my family. As I get better at preparing for the future, I become more optimistic about the future and more peaceful in the present.

CHAPTER 19

CAN HUMANS DO WHAT PROFITS SAY?

We have to be able to live in the moment and plan ahead. Allow yourself to be driven by faith instead of fear. To live in faith, you must first realize how much of your perspectives and actions are driven by fear. Take a minute to observe yourself from a distance. Analyze and ask yourself, how much of what I do is driven by fear? For instance, do you wake up extra early for work in fear of being late? Or can you find a reasonable time to wake up that gives you plenty of time to get ready, without rushing, to make it to work on time? Now instead of rushing and speed walking every morning, you can take your time and trust that you will make it to work on time at a constant slow and steady pace. You can do this without any fear of the consequences for being late. You can start your day in a peaceful state of mind, worry free, for the entire duration of your journey on the way to work. I understand it's an entirely separate challenge to stay peaceful and worry free once you get to work.

Live with trust in the universe and in yourself. Believe that if you do the right thing, everything will be okay in the long run. Go with your gut feeling of doing what's right. It's difficult to put into words what that gut feeling feels like, but I can usually tell the difference from when something feels right to when something feels wrong.

Start with simple things. Does it feel right to eat breakfast when you wake up, or are you still sustained from yesterday's dinner? Does it feel right to wake up a little early tomorrow to avoid traffic, or do you feel you can sleep a little longer and take your time in the morning while getting ready for work? Does it feel right to call your mother on her birthday and tell her you love her or to avoid your responsibility on that day?

Do what you feel is the right thing to do, and everything will be okay. Trust and have faith in this way of living and seeing the world. Anxiety and depression are the result of not living with trust and faith in yourself and in the universe.

The reality is that no one is perfect. What is that thing that makes me want more things? Is it my ego? My insecurities? Is it my craving for approval from others? For example, I'll see a leather jacket that I like. It's reasonably priced. So I try it on. Of course, it fits, and now I want it. But then I think about how much money I have left in the bank. I have enough to get this leather jacket, but then I wouldn't have enough money for cigarettes and food to get me to the next paycheck. I really consider buying the jacket anyway because I believe that if I don't buy this now, it won't be here in a couple weeks when I have enough money. It takes me a while to put it back on the rack and walk away.

Putting the jacket back is a mature decision. The younger careless me would have said, "Fuck it," and bought it anyway and deal with the consequences later. Who cares? I got what I want. But those are selfish and irresponsible attitudes. I have realized that this selfish way of behaving gets me nowhere in life. Maybe I have some nice material things, but I'm alone. And when I'm alone, I become self-destructive.

Even after making the mature decision of putting the jacket back, I still think about it for the next few days. I am aware that I have obsessive qualities. When I like something, I obsess over it, and that's not always a good thing. I'm still trying to figure out how to control it. The first action is recognizing it when it shows up. The second action is challenging/outsmarting the negative thinking and not to give into it. The last action is believing I made the right decision.

Why do desires have to be so attractive? I literally feel a magnetic pull toward the things I like and want. My problem is wanting things that I don't need. I know I don't need it; I only want it. But why do I want it? This wanting could be anything. Do I want it to show off and impress the people around me? As strange as it sounds, I think I like impressing strangers more than I like impressing my friends and family. With friends and family, I want to feel equal with them—also with the people I work with. I don't feel a need to be better than them. I want to impress them but with my work performance not with what I'm wearing.

Even still, what is this thing that makes me want things I don't need? Can I trace this back to my childhood? When I would kick and scream for some new toy I wanted? Does the mentality of seven-year-old me still live inside the thirty-six-year-old me? Aren't those the years of my beginning stages of ego development developing this obsessive side of me that wants everything in the world, one toy at a time? Eventually, I put the toys down because of my developing interest and curiosity for girls. At the very least, I must be able to recognize my obsessive tendencies when they begin. If I don't catch it early, I find myself on the way to go get more things I don't need.

During my late teenage years and in my early twenties, my work responsibilities were to clean and to make the more experienced guys' lives easier. The way I saw it, it was like Jim Morrison sweeping your floor. This attitude and perspective was the biggest challenge in my life to overcome. It took me many years to understand and respect the ladder of advancement.

Step back from the movie of life. We must work hard for everything we have. Focus on the moment-to-moment aspect of "what is the next thing I should do right now?". Eventually, you will get to the finish line. Then a new journey will appear. I try to step way back and observe my world from a distance because every now and then I get caught up in the trivial details of my life.

At the movies, we forget we are in a theater. We are watching the assortment of lights flicker on the movie screen. Without the flickering lights creating the illusion of a movie scene, it's just a blank screen. Just as in life, we are captivated by light and vibrating molecules and atoms. We forgot about the world outside of the "movie" we are watching.

What matters to you? What is important to you? Because the matter that you deem important becomes alive. Whatever matter at hand you feel is important becomes your entire world. It becomes the only thing that you can see. Kids and adults want social acceptance from their peer group. That's why we wear the clothes we wear and act the way we act—because of what is acceptable in our social circles.

What is our purpose? Weren't we meant for more? Meant for more than to just work, raise a family, pay bills, and die? Occasionally we get a vacation and brief moments of fun and genuine enjoyment. But we don't have a major war to fight. Our war is our daily battle within ourselves. Maybe there are some people that are lucky and don't really have any inner demons. But I think a lot of us do. Many of my friends have a traumatic past that haunts them. Bad things happen to good people. We must deal with it, and we all deal with it differently. After I had enough of life beating me up, I turned to self-destruction. The subconscious thinking was *If I have to go through some suffering, I'm doing it my way.* Self-destruction starts off as fun and provides instant relief. After some time, it starts to hurt. It hurt me physically and emotionally and took all my valuable possessions away including all the money I had saved over time.

We are getting smarter as modern human beings and, in turn, becoming more depressed. I want more out of my life than just being a worker bee serving the queen then dying. I don't want to be seventy years old when I retire. I want to enjoy my life and share it with my friends and family. I want to teach and pass on what I have learned because I feel that I've lived numerous lives within this lifetime. I have a lot of information, experience, and knowledge to share; and I want to share it with more than just my family.

I seek out answers to life's complicated questions. What good are the answers if I can't or don't share them? I can't be that selfish. Most people ask the same complicated questions when they become adults and are thrown into this cold world. Let's face it, once you're an adult, you're on your own. Who is here to teach us how to continue on? Who will teach the teacher? Who will lead the leader? At this point in my life, I can no longer rely on my parents to bail me out of the problems I face.

We are led by an inner driving force. Some call it the human soul. Some call it God. Either way, we are connected to something divine and infinite. It doesn't communicate like you and me. It speaks through a sort of telekinesis. Sometimes certain situations and events can be translated to a message. A message that was transmitted by the universe for you to observe and conclude the meaning.

You get what you give. If you see the world as a dark and cold place, that's what it will be for you. If you see the world as warm and generous, that's what it will be for you. Ultimately, we decide and create our own individual reality through the choices we make, big and small. Through our perspective and our awareness, we are choosing to view the world the way we want to see it. The perspectives we have are not always a conscious decision. Some of our perspectives have been programmed into our subconscious at an early age.

Step back for a moment and observe yourself and your life. What are you not okay with? Ask yourself if you have the ability to change or fix the things that you are not okay with. What would you like to improve? Ask yourself if you have the ability to improve it. Ask the universe (God) for the courage and the strength to make the little improvements necessary to your well-being, and be patient with the progress. After some time and discipline, you will see the results. Find contentment in realizing that you have everything you need. Allow your maturity to crystalize. Accept that you can't get everything you want right away. But anything you put your attention to will naturally start to materialize. It starts with attention, intention, and focusing your awareness on taking that first step toward fulfilling your desire.

How do I get over my trauma and numerous heartbreaks? I have come to believe that those experiences have only made me stronger and wiser. Instead of running from those difficult experiences, I fully embrace them as part of myself. I didn't like it then and still don't like that it happened, but I must draw a lesson out of it. Now I can reach out to the next heart that is broken and assist them through their pain because I have gone through a very similar pain. We are able to relate to each other. By opening up and telling my story, they feel more comfortable to open up and tell their story. Just by talking and letting it out, the emotional pain is lifted slightly. We are relating to each other on an emotional level, and relating to another human being is a great place for true healing to begin.

How do I believe in myself after I have failed so many times? I have come to believe that giving up is the only failure. Every time I have fallen, I get back up. Some falls took a little longer, but I always get back up. Each time I get back up, I become stronger. Getting back up hurts, but I work through the pain and keep going. That's the focus. Keep going. Have faith that you will only get better with time and experience. You learn and grow more from failures than you do with success.

As I look back, I can clearly see my progress. I gain confidence by realizing how far I've come. I give myself permission to be satisfied with myself and stop agreeing with thoughts that tell me I should be depressed and unfulfilled. I identify changes that I can make that will improve my quality of life and make a promise to myself to take the necessary actions that will bring about these changes. Even if I only take one step today, even if it's only one small action, I know that I am one more step closer to reaching the goal. I no longer allow myself to procrastinate and, in turn, deny myself happiness.

One example, I wanted to get back in shape. So I promised myself I would work out at least two times every week. If I was feeling up for it and I had the energy, three times a week. After a couple weeks of discipline, I could clearly see the results, and I became more satisfied with myself. My confidence grew, and my outlook on the future became brighter.

Learning from our mistakes is like repairing a broken bone with titanium. Whereas the broken bone is the mistake, and the titanium is the lesson learned. The bone that was broken is now stronger than it ever was, and it looks beautiful with a marbled titanium. This is also a metaphor for your psyche and inner well-being. We become stronger and more beautiful on the inside by helping those who are going through a similar suffering that we went through. Wisdom is stillness. There is a deep knowing within yourself, and on the outside, you are perfectly and comfortably still.

CHAPTER 20

THE WALK HOME FROM SCHOOL IN SEVENTH GRADE

One day after school during my seventh-grade year of junior high school, I decided to walk home instead of taking the bus like I usually did. I would say it's about a three-mile walk. It took roughly forty-five minutes. But as an eleven-year-old, that seemed like an impossible journey to embark on. Before I started walking, it seemed like a great idea. I felt like I lived close enough to the school to walk home. Maybe I was sick of taking the bus too.

Whatever I was thinking quickly changed once I realized how long this walk would be. To speed things up, I think I tried running for a little while. But I remember stopping in my tracks, breaking down, and crying. I was upset with myself and the decision I had made. I promised myself that I would never walk home from school again. But I had to get through this journey I was on. I couldn't turn around and go back to the school to catch another bus. There were no other buses to catch. I couldn't call anyone to pick me up. There were no cell phones at the time, only beepers. I had to just keep walking until I got home. I remember trying to distract myself while walking by singing songs.

After about twenty minutes into this walk, I was halfway home. I started to feel better and more confident that I could make it. At the beginning of this walk, I don't remember the exact reason why

I was so upset that it brought me to tears. Did I think that I would die? Did I think that I didn't possess the ability to walk for that long of a distance? I do remember that I was scared and that I had felt very alone and very far from home. At the time, this was the longest walk I went on by myself. I had taken plenty of walks through the back roads of my neighborhood and through the woods that led to a little strip mall. But this walk home from school seemed a million times longer than that. It was probably more like twice the distance compared to the walk through the woods.

I am bringing up this long walk home from junior high school because I believe it sparked something inside me after I finally made it home. I felt like I had completed an impossible task all by myself at a young age. I made the decision by myself, and I saw it through. No one was waiting for me at home. I had no one to impress. No one was challenging me. It was not a race. I just wanted to walk home instead of taking the bus. Although, the bus can be a socially uncomfortable place if you don't have anyone to hang out with. At the start of the walk, I wanted to give up. But I didn't. I just kept going. I figured out ways to calm myself down while still making forward progress.

This feels like a metaphor for my life at the current moment. I'm on this journey. Even though I have been walking for a long time, I still feel like I have a long way to go. Sometimes I want to give up, stop going forward, curl up in a ball, and cry. But I don't. I just keep going. Sometimes I have to figure out how to distract myself or calm myself down to keep making forward progress. All I want is to make it home safely. Right now, I don't know where home is. Home is the metaphor for the goal I am striving for, like getting a raise and a promotion in my career. Getting married and having a baby or two. Saving enough money to be able to support my family. Setting up a retirement fund so I don't have to work my entire life. Publishing a book. Creating music. Selling a painting. Owning property.

I feel like I have a few good ideas to become successful during this lifetime, but I keep getting in my own way. I have such trouble saving the money I make. So until I become a responsible adult, I'm going to keep going around and around in circles. It's similar to me turning around and giving up on my long walk home, trying to reverse my initial decision to go on this long journey by myself. Sometimes I want to give up so someone else can pick me up and carry me home. But there is no one here to do that. The people around me are relying on me to carry them. I keep telling myself, and I'm telling you, just keep going. Eventually you will make it. Your bright future is waiting for you if you continue to make good decisions that benefit you and everyone around you.

CHAPTER 21

PATIENCE AND WAITING

Patience and waiting. That's the most difficult part of going through the daily maintenance and work that life requires while, at the same time, waiting to reach your goals. Big and small, long-term and short-term. I don't think anyone enjoys waiting, especially me. I keep telling myself, "Don't worry. Your bright future is waiting for you. Take a break when you need it, but just keep going. Continue to follow your dreams and always do the right thing."

I believe our general purpose is to learn, practice, and teach. Then repeat. Not everybody is okay to devoting their life to being a poor righteous teacher. Most people are on the search for something or someone. I've been told many times to appreciate the things I have and stop putting most of my focus on what I don't have. I do appreciate what I have, but sometimes I feel so teased by the rich and advertisers. They make me want the things I don't have. I want the big house, the nice car, the model wife, the high-fashion wardrobe, the high-paying job, and all the swagger and confidence that comes along with it.

If we haven't learned this lesson already, we eventually will: that the things that you own eventually end up owning you. Our obsession over material things becomes greater than our appreciation for our loving relationships and for the amazing gift of life. There must be a way to be happy and content without being rich and owning the world. Obviously, we need some basic things to survive and to at least be comfortable. We must reach a happy medium. We have to meet in the middle somewhere between a spiritual mystic and a business tycoon. Our wishes and desires must be realistic and unselfish.

But we are not perfect, so occasionally, we are going to want something extravagant. Where does this wanting and craving come from? The constant wanting could be a result of feeling incomplete. A subconscious feeling that I don't matter. A feeling of not being loved or accepted. Not feeling acceptance from myself or from others. Why would I feel that way? Who makes me feel that way? Was it from getting my heart broken? Is it from not feeling very close to my parents? Is it from feeling like an outcast in high school? Is it from my jealousy of the rich? Is it from the envy of my bosses at work that are near retirement? Is it my resentment that I may have to work until I'm seventy years old? Is it from my anger at myself that I have not saved enough money to buy a house yet? Is it from the damage I've done to myself from years of alcohol and drug abuse?

I can list more things, but I'm going to stop there. I have many reasons to feel incomplete and insecure and, overall, just not good enough and not deserving of the good life. Maybe I subconsciously self-sabotage myself to keep myself at this low stage in life. At some point I have to say "Enough is enough" and "Today is the day I make changes for the better." No longer will I continue this self-destructive behavior. I have to accept that there will be withdrawals. My brain will try to tell me to continue the negative behavior because that's what we know and we are comfortable here lying in self-pity. I have to recognize these thoughts early enough to stop them and to not give in to them. Keep the promise you made to yourself. I promise that I will get myself healthy again and get back on track so that I can continue to take care of my family and myself.

How do we explain tragedy? Of course, there is the dictionary definition. But I want to freestyle my own definition. Or maybe give some examples to help define the tragedy that I am thinking of now. Wasted talent is a tragedy. A good man getting taken advantage of by a beautiful and selfish young woman is a tragedy. Family members that do not speak to one another over petty bullshit that happened a long time ago is a tragedy. Innocent children getting hooked on drugs is a tragedy. Not going for your very-reachable dream is a tragedy. Settling for less than what you know is your value is a tragedy. What is stopping us from truly chasing our dreams? Fear of failure is at the top of that list.

I have the ability to wake up, get up, get dressed, and go to work. That ability is the starting point of me making money. I have realized that this is a strength and a strong quality I've developed over the years of going to work. The first time I realized this strength, it energized me on the way to work. It may sound silly to some, but I feel these realizations are important to our growth as individuals. I'm sure in some way, it has happened to you as well. All of a sudden, you realize something. And the realization of this something has a lasting impact on you.

I have also realized that during my downtime or free time that my mind produces self-destructive thoughts and ideas. Through the years of repeating bad habits, I've created these thought pathways in my mind. They appear like an uncontrollable reflex. It is now my responsibility to recognize this when it happens and why this happens then challenge the negative thought by not following through with it because that is not who I am anymore.

Perfection represents all that is holy, pure, and balanced. We as human beings can aim for that direction. I have come to believe that perfection is a direction, not a destination. We have demons to recognize and confront, and we must not give into the temptation of evil.

Who you believe you are must match with "what is" in your personal reality. This is where balance and peace in the mind occurs. This was an important concept for me to understand. I truly believe this is correct. It is difficult to reach 100-percent balance. That would mean perfection in all areas of your life. I strive for at least 51 percent favored in my belief of who I am to what my personal reality actually is. An aligning belief of who I am is as follows: I believe that I have artistic talents, but my career is not of a professional artist selling million-dollar paintings. But I paint on canvas in my free time. Some of my paintings I give away, and some I hang on my walls. I am still able to keep my artistic talents a part of my life even though it is not how I make a living.

An existing conflicting belief of who I am is as follows: I believe that I am an addict in recovery. I also have a belief that I could get away with getting a little high sometimes. These beliefs generate thoughts that tug me in two opposite directions. When I make a decision, one of those beliefs fade away. Even though they are conflicting beliefs of who I am, I am still able to make the right decision in favor of what is best for me.

Is free time really free? Even though we may have nothing to do at the moment, we are spending the time doing something. Even if that something is nothing, the time is still being spent. I cannot produce artwork on demand. That's not how it works for me. There is a creative energy that builds up over some time, and then it's released. Sometimes I don't paint or write anything for weeks. At other times, I am working on something just about every day. If I try to force something creatively, it never comes out right. When I paint or write, I'm not thinking about the next move. The words just flow out of me. I control my hands, but during those moments, I'm not really trying to control my hands. I allow them to move on their own. This is hard to explain in words, but it is most commonly referred to as "being in the zone."

When the room is quiet, I can hear this steady ring in my ears. The pitch and tone changes very slightly. But it's always there. I kind of like it. It's soothing in a way. Is it the sound of my radar or awareness? It definitely has something to do with my sense of hearing. So I appreciate it being here. I'm just curious as to what it is exactly. Is it similar to the buzzing sound that light fixtures make? Because I've heard that's an electrical phenomenon. Or is it the sound of the electric current circulating through my brain?

CHAPTER 22

CHILDHOOD

Why did I smash the pirate ship made of Legos? One of my earliest memories is, as a little boy, building a Lego pirate ship with my Dad. It was a big ship made up of many small pieces, and it took us hours to build. Then when we were done, I took the ship back to my room when no one was looking and I destroyed it. I threw it down to the floor so hard that it smashed into pieces.

After all this time, I'm still not sure why. I can only guess that I enjoy destroying and breaking things. Is that one of our primal instincts? But once I realized what I had done, I was so remorseful, so upset with myself. I was disappointed in myself that I had destroyed something beautiful my dad and I had built. I remember crying. I cried because I was so confused with myself and couldn't understand why I did what I did. Somehow it was put back together because I remember playing with it again later on. I had it on display in my room for a long time after that. I cherished that pirate ship once it was put back together again.

How can I translate this as my subconscious? I am that pirate ship. That pirate ship is me. That pirate ship is my relationship between me and my dad. Was I mad at him for not spending enough time with me? There must have been some kind of brewing pain within me that caused me to do that as a physical expression of my frustration.

This happens again many years later, but this time I destroy my own life. Did I build myself up just to tear it down? Just to see what it would be like to destroy a beautiful life? My own life? The one I know best? Was I testing how much destruction and chaos I could take without dying? But still, why? Why do I enjoy destruction? Is that a primal instinct? Am I bored when things are going well? Do I enjoy building just to destroy and destroying just to build back up again?

If I neglect what I am supposed to maintain, it will deteriorate on its own. If I want my life to continue on an upward trajectory, I have to maintain it on a regular basis. If I could understand this question of why I like to destroy, then I would be able to understand the inner workings of myself much clearer. Right now, I'm okay. But I must maintain my well-being to remain this way. Because for me, a little destructive streak will turn into a long unstoppable destructive streak.

Who did you have to be for your parents as a kid? Who did you have to be for your teachers and classmates? Who did you have to be for your friends outside of school? Are you still that person now? For my parents, I had to set a well-behaved example for my brother and sisters. To keep my parents from being disappointed in me, I had to maintain an A average in school. To be accepted at school and considered cool, I had to look like a movie star. If I didn't look cool, I was seen as a loser by the girls I liked.

Can you see that the bar is set very high for kids just starting junior high school? Can you see that if I did not meet the expectations of my parents and the kids I went to school with that I would be crushed by embarrassment and an overwhelming sense that I am not good enough? I believe that this sense of feeling "not good enough" is carried through into my adulthood. I've noticed that the high school mentality and the popularity contests are also present at the workplace.

I was sent to my room a lot when I was a kid. I spent a lot of time alone. I can't say that I didn't have a good childhood. I did have a good childhood. But I can say I was tormented—tormented by the same people I cared about and craved the approval of.

While I was alone, I played with my toys. Mostly action figures of He-Man, Ghostbusters, Batman, the X-Men, etc. I created fight scenes with my imagination. I built pirate ships and castles out of

Legos. I collected toy guns, and I always created a scene where the good guy (me) had to overcome an obstacle or disagreement with the bad guy (my tormentors).

My collection of things translates to my collection of relationships and the approval I was seeking from them. I always searched for the next best thing. There was always another toy I wanted. When I finally got that new action figure or gun, which was usually on birthdays or Christmas, I would covet that toy. I protected that toy. I put it up on a pedestal or hid it for safekeeping. Then I searched for the next awesome toy. This translates to my subconscious mind as always searching for the next best thing because the things that I did have was not good enough. That I was not good enough. This is a very dangerous mindset that was carried into my drinking and drugging.

Throughout my entire life I have always felt the pressure of having to constantly improve. Self-improvement was not explained very well to my gullible mind. Again, it translated into my subconscious as "Get more, be more" because I was not enough, I was not complete.

The first physical activity I participated in was karate while I was in third grade. The beginners are given the white belt. I quickly realized that there were many more colors of belts to go through before reaching the black belt. I saw the red belts practicing together, and I immediately set my sights on becoming one of them. But the red belt was five tiers away from my white belt. Realistically, it would have taken me about three to five years to earn the red belt. But of course, I wanted it now! And since I couldn't get it now, I became discouraged very quickly and gave up.

CHAPTER 23

GRANDPARENTS AND GOD

I believe my grandparents are close. So close that I have the ability to summon their strength and encouragement. I have come to believe that my grandparents live on through me. I wear my grandfather's medals and achievements he earned from the Marines. I carry them with me with pride. I follow his orders and pick up where he left off. In the name of my grandparents, I vow to continue to learn and continue to grow, expanding my inclusiveness and in my understanding.

Grandma Rizzo, I will raise a family. Just like you.

Grandpa Allen, I will build. Just like you. I will put my kids and grandkids through college. Just like you.

Grandma Allen, I will believe in and follow God. Just like you.

Grandpa Rizzo, I will love and bring joy. Just like you.

My heroes are all ghosts. They are watching me with all their eyes and what I seem to value most.

What I am saying here is not the end all, be all. This is how I see it. This is what I have come to believe. I am not asking anyone to agree with me. I am only putting into words my perspective on, what I consider to be, God.

God is creation. God is intelligence. Intelligence is omnipresent. Every particle of this existence is brimming with intelligence. The seed knows when to sprout, and the flower knows when to bloom. All of life that is exists in this creation is expressing that infinite intelligence. When you begin to behold this living phenomenon taking place all around you, all your questions start dissolving into an over-whelming sense of wonder. That is the true art of living.

I have come to believe that most religions have the same message. Do unto others as you would have others do unto you. In other words, don't fuck with me, and I won't fuck with you. It doesn't matter how you get the message or who delivers it. The important question is, did you get the message?

The reason it is difficult to define God is because every person has their own unique take on what God is or is not or if God exists at all. If we were going to have a conversation about God, then every-one involved must be able to consider other possibilities other than their own beliefs. Otherwise, we cannot have a healthy philosophical discussion about what God is or is not. When discussing what God is, I believe that there is no right or wrong answer. Only possibilities. Only potential.

For me, I do not see God as an old bearded man in the sky. I cannot see God, but I can see what God has created. I view God as the intelligence of the universe. Planet Earth is within the universe, and we are all included within planet Earth. Everything is connected to everything. Can you see intelligence? Is intelligence a tangible thing you can hold in your hand? I would say no. But we can sense it. When I say intelligence, I mean things like what is the force that holds up the planets and sun? No human I know can hold up the sun. This would be a power greater than ourselves. Some scientists may say that forces of gravity hold up the sun and its orbiting plan-ets. That may be true. But I take the explanation defined by humans and say God is holding up the sun. There is an amazing, powerful yet subtle force at work here. That same amazing, powerful yet sub-tle force is within all living things, all elements, and all materials of nature. Including us.

When asking spiritual questions, I work backward to find an answer. I ask myself, "Where did I come from?" Most directly, I was made by my parents. My parents were made from their parents, which are my grandparents. Now the answer has doubled because what was two has just become four. I could continue to trace back my lineage, but instead I will look at all humans starting from the beginning of our existence on this planet. The first humans lived off the land; they survived by cultivating what the earth provided us. Since the first humans were dependent on the plants and animals to survive, we can safely assume that plants and animals were here before humans. A big part of our physical composition is made from what we ingest, also including what we breathe. It makes sense to me that humans evolved from animals over the course of millions of years.

Where did plants and animals come from? They were made from the elements of earth. The elements of our planet are air, water, fire, and earth (rock minerals). Before there were many different forms of life existing on this planet, there was only air, water, fire, and minerals. There is a theory for the origin of life that I have come to respect as a very possible truth. And that is that the first form of life came from the depths of the ocean, deep within the volcanos. The perfect combination of the water from the ocean, fire from the volcano, rocks, minerals, and a bubble of air. These volcanos were submerged deep in the ocean, so when this newly formed life bubble was pushed out of the volcano, it was born into the waters of our ocean.

This life bubble evolved from a single-celled living organism into a fish that could swim over the course of millions of years. After a few more million years, that fish was able to walk on land and breathe the air. That first life-form that was able to walk on land and breathe the air went on to evolve into every other animal life-form on this planet, including human beings.

Continuing with working backward, the elements came from planet Earth. The earth was born from our universe. Our Milky Way universe was born from exploding stars, the dust particles from those exploding stars, and the forces of our universe, which is gravity, electromagnetism, and weak and strong nuclear forces. These forces are created and maintained by what I consider to be God. By inference, I was made from these forces. Every form of life that I have ever known has come from these forces. These forces live within me. The same forces that hold up the sun hold me up as well. Human beings are electric. There is a steady current of electricity flowing through all of us. The same electricity that's in lightning. When lightning strikes, the boom of a sound it makes is thunder. Our thunder is our voice. Are you getting goose bumps? Are the hairs standing up on your arms and on the back of your neck? Are you beginning to feel your connection to the powerful forces of the universe?

Can we see gravity? No, but we can see the result of gravity. So we know it's there. The same is true for God. Since God is the creator of the forces of the universe and since the forces of the universe do not have a defined boundary of a physical shape, how could I even begin to define a shape for God?

CHAPTER 24

THE NEW YORK EXPERIMENT

The New York experiment is the experiment of seeing if people from all over the world could live together in harmony. Are we succeeding? Is it a success? Is it a failure?

In my opinion, it is both, but it is also a work in progress. It is a success because immigrants have built one of the biggest, wealthiest, and most-populated cities in the world. It is a failure because of the racism, the fighting, the poverty, the hunger, and the fact that most people step over the homeless rather than stretch out a helping hand. Literally and figuratively. New York is the city you come to make your dreams a reality because New York has everything and within walking distance. But no one will help you get there. All within the same street corner you will see beauty, ugliness, peace, violence, the rich, the poor, cleanliness, and filth. Is it no coincidence that what many people call the greatest city in the world is inhabited with people from all over the world?

Everyone comes here to create a better life for themselves. A true multicultural, multiracial, democratic society. But we can't see past our own selfishness. Everyone has their own agenda, their own beliefs, and their own way of life. If we would simply accept all people and everything about them, I believe we would create harmony. But the rich control the city by keeping the little guy down and making the middle class pay all the taxes. Racism tears us apart. Hate and distrust divides.

If you want to see change, be the change you want to see, right? You know what happens if I'm too nice? Everyone will walk all over me and take advantage any way they can. Yes, it's important to lead by example, but we also have to spread this message. It is not enough to lead by example and say nothing. We are all racing to strike it rich and will step over anyone that gets in our way. We don't take breaks; we work through lunch. Do you know how fast a New York minute is? Barely even thirty seconds. We are striving to become the very thing we despise: untouchably wealthy. Plenty of us have heard of this dream coming true for enough people to make us believe it could come true for us if we work hard enough. If we are clever enough. If we come up with the right gimmick, we could strike it rich in New York.

I don't believe this mentality will go away anytime soon. But I do believe that New Yorkers will become wiser and more respectful of each other. I want to see New Yorkers that work only during work hours, not sixteen-hour workdays. I want New York bosses respecting their employees' time off the clock. I want to see shelters built for the homeless and those shelters staffed with social workers and addiction counselors. I want Alcoholics Anonymous signs to be proudly displayed on the buildings where the meetings are being held. Mainly because if you don't know anyone in AA, it is very difficult to find a meeting. I want the rich to pay a fair amount of taxes, not none of the taxes. I want the police to serve and protect, not harass the people. We can agree that the career of a police officer is not an easy one. Maybe it's their training that is in need of an update. Maybe it's the hiring process. Maybe the police should not be responsible for writing a certain number of tickets to make their quota. There should be no quota. The police should not be forced to write tickets to make a full weeks' pay. The police should not be responsible for performing drug raids.

We all know that there is plenty of evil to around. A police officer's main objective should be to protect the public from danger. I don't think anyone has any issues with the fire department. Those men and women are amazing the way they run toward danger to save another life. I wish the police were given similar responsibilities as the fire department is given. Everything that I just listed here are not expensive wishes. I believe these are things that our government could make happen relatively quickly. The remaining wishes are up to the people of New York. So what's it gonna be? I am you, and you are me.

Sometime in the near future, all races will melt into one race. We will no longer be black, brown, or white. We will be evolved human beings. This is the moment when racism disappears. Judgment placed upon any one human being will be from not what they look like but from their character.

Don't give up on us. I have come to believe that any one person can turn their life around for the better because I've seen it happen many times. Many friends of mine have gotten sober and repaired all the damage done and have built a new life on a strong foundation. I believe that if I can do it, anyone can do it because I was every part of a hopeless alcoholic and addict. I overdosed numerous times. I burned many bridges, broke any trust that anyone had in me, ruined all relationships, spent all my money and sold everything I had. But through my dedication and perseverance, I repaired it all. My one seed of faith that I had in myself to be restored back to sanity kept me going. Don't give up on us. Believe in us. We need your faith in us just as much as we need faith in ourselves.

CHAPTER 25

CONSCIOUSNESS

There are many theories, ideas, and beliefs on what consciousness is. Synonyms for consciousness are *focus*, *attention*, and *awareness*. How long can you focus on one thing? How long can you keep your attention and listen to one full conversation? How many pages of a book can you read before forgetting what you just read? Can you watch an entire movie without losing focus? Without thinking of something else? How long can you pay attention to what someone is saying before zoning out for a few moments?

To me, consciousness is my awareness and attention. Can you see consciousness? No, it's omnipresent. It's everywhere and nowhere at the same time. My consciousness is the real me. The real me is not my body or my mind. The real me is not my emotions or my thoughts. I am not the contents in the room. I am the space of the room where all contents exist. Mystics use the movie screen analogy when explaining consciousness. They start by explaining that before the movie starts, all you have is a blank screen. Then the light from the projector shines onto the movie screen. The movie is literally made of microscopic particles of light and color. While watching the movie, everything else around the movie screen falls away. The seats disappear, the audience disappears, your own body and mind disappears. Your consciousness submerges itself in the movie. You become the movie. Sometimes we forget that we are even watching a movie. It's not real, but we believe that it is real. In this analogy, the movie are the events of your own personal life.

I have beliefs that are so ingrained, so habitual, such a reflex that I don't even realize that they are there and that these ingrained beliefs are controlling and forming my perspectives and thoughts and in turn affecting my emotions. To find wisdom, I must be willing to let go myself, face loneliness and fear, and resist the temptation to grab for relief. I must be willing to let go of the illusion I have of myself with the intention of discovering my full potential as a spiritual being. I must drop the parts of me that have been holding me back from where I so desperately want to go. I need to push open the door to my life and, every day, bite off more than I can chew and chew it. I cannot heal what I conceal. I am not responsible for my first thought, but I am responsible for the second thought. It is possible for the observer to become the observed, the experiencer to become the experience. Do not create the division of subject and object. This division is the root cause of misery.

Spiritually wise men/women do not know many things, but they are sure of one thing: that they are not the body or the mind. To be successful in this life, we must understand the unity of everything. As an adult, we struggle to regain a similar connection like we had with our mother in the womb. The root problem of the inner psyche is that it doesn't feel whole and complete within itself. It seeks something or someone to make it feel complete. If left unattended, the mind can spin out into perpetual absurdity. Live life instead of fearing it. Don't buy into what your mind is telling you to do to make everything okay. The truth is, everything will be okay as soon as you are okay with everything, and that's the only time everything will be okay.

The action to take is relax and release. The mind follows the heart. The heart reacts way before the mind starts talking. At some point in your spiritual journey, you will allow your heart to lead the way. The mind doesn't even get a chance to start up because you let go at the heart level.

The psyche was built upon avoiding pain, and as a result, the fear of pain is at its foundation. Do not devote your life to avoiding physical or psychological pain. If you want to be free, view inner pain as a temporary shift in your energy. There is no reason to fear this experience. The truth is pain is the price to freedom. All this stored pain must go to find the presence of God within you.

Become aware of a universe behind your seat of consciousness. You will walk through every moment of your daily life with the flow of this inner force sustaining you and guiding you deep within. The greatest gift you can give to God is to be pleased with his/her creation. God has created the heavens and earth so that he/she can experience himself/herself through us.

Our personal problems are not serious problems, such as a fatal illness. Our personal problems are just events that take place on earth. There is nothing to deal with except for our own fears and desires. An individual sunbeam is no different from the sun. If its consciousness stopped identifying itself as the beam, it comes to know itself as the sun.

The mind will become quiet when we ask, "Who am I?" and "To whom has this thought arisen?" A thought or emotion comes from either the light from within or from the shadows outside. Which one of these did this thought or emotion come from? It is either from fear or from love. From separateness or unity.

The basis of all building blocks of atoms and life-forms is of one dot orbiting another dot, which forms a circle. Our divine purpose is to find our way back to God. To become one with the Holy Spirit, which, for a time, happens when we die. And I believe, it also happens when we dream. Can we become one with the Holy Spirit during this lifetime? Are we are somewhat limited by our physical form?

God was given to you to remind you of what you are. You are love. You were made from love. Love is who you are. Your ability to love is based on your willingness to include everything in your environment. God can only observe without judgment. Inner peace is not the final goal. Inner peace is the road to all goals worth pursuing. God does not punish. But he gave us the ability and the option to punish ourselves or to take care of ourselves.

Shift your vision and perception away from anger. Anger is a sign that you are focusing on limited or illusory aspects to justify your judgments. We get very upset when we see something that is not really there because of our creative imagination. It's not about how hard you can hit. It's about how hard you can get hit then get back up. It's not about winning or losing. It's about playing the game. Recognize the greatness within you and deliver it. To express how we think and feel is a basic human need. Your mind is like a radio, and your hand is on the dial, controlling the frequency. Turn the dial consciously. It's important that we let go of our resentments. Having resentment is like drinking poison and hoping that it will kill the other person.

After heartbreak, my unconscious thoughts sounded like this: *Look at me! I am dying because of you!* I thought this as I metaphorically slit my own wrists. These thoughts must change to *Look at me now. Because of you I have lived.* With this change in perspective, we go from death to life. Give the heartbreaker credit for helping you. They are not devils; they are angels. The experience of heartbreak makes you stronger and wiser. Yes, it hurts at first, and for me, I felt the pain for years. But now I'm a better person because of what I went through. I have a better understanding of relationships. I have a better understanding of what to do and what not to do. I learned how to see the one I love not as my property, but as an independent person. We join together every day by choice.

The original sin was simply an error in perception when Adam took a bite of the apple offered by the devil. God explicitly told him not to eat the forbidden apples, and the devil tempted him with those same apples. The apples went from forbidden to something delicious and desirable. Adam went from unity with God to separation from God because the devil made him see the apples in a different way. There was an identity shift. That is the point at which the sin begins. This identity shift happens every time you wake up from sleeping and identify with your body, ego, and what you see as your problems.

Know yourself. Not as a body and a mind but as a spiritual being, a divine being. Make the conscious shift from separation to unity. Reclaim your original innocence. This is one of the main reasons why we are here. We are in the pursuit of heaven in exchange for going through hell. The body is the means by which God's son returns to sanity. The ego wages war against the spirit. But the Holy Spirit uses the ego or intellect as a vehicle for the expression of love. The ego makes a lousy master but an extraordinary servant.

Is something preventing me from engaging in helping the next person in need? Is it my fear of rejection? My fear of you not accepting my help? Is it my fear of your perception of me? How do I get over this and see past it? I have found it very helpful to see yourself in other people. See yourself as the other person. You were just like them in their time of need. See the innocent divine being in all people.

A closed heart leads to lethargy. An open heart unleashes the energy of the soul. You can open your heart by way of trust. Trust the situation, trust the person, trust yourself, trust in God. Open your heart with enthusiasm. The most common fear is fear of failure and fear of rejection. We become driven by this fear and identify with forms and material things to feel safe and secure. As we begin to identify with these things, they become the definition of who we are. The more we define ourselves with things, the more we separate from God. Be in a constant state of letting go of the pull that the energy of this distraction has on your consciousness.

The ego is the masquerading self. We have pulled the mask of the ego over ourselves to define ourselves, to keep ourselves oriented in this ever-changing world. The underlying emotion is fear—fear that you will lose the things you identify with, that everything will go wrong. And we sell ourselves and everyone else this ego every day. That's why we get our hair cut. That's why we shower and wear nice clothes. We become control freaks, clinging to objects to identify ourselves. Are we dealing with the core or dealing with the facade? We must deal with our core selves instead of hiding from ourselves through identifying with our things and, in turn, easily becoming disturbed. We have a hypersensitive psyche. We put up a psychological protective shield. This shield is locking your illness inside yourself and will only get worse. Understand that if you are using this metaphorical shield to protect yourself, you will never be free. You would be locking in a scared, insecure person within your heart.

We cling to good and bad experiences. Good experiences are clung to, and bad experiences get pushed down inside. This is physically draining because it takes much more energy to not let it go. Decide not to live blocked from inner peace. Deal with the little things. Let them go as soon as they come up. As you let go, you become stronger. Allow pain and anxiety to pass through your heart. You may get disturbed, but that's okay. Let it come, then let it go. It will go if you trust that it will go. Keep your heart strong by letting go and releasing each thought and emotion. We struggle in life because we are trying to cling to things that are not permanent.

Allow reality to just be. Accept it as it is. Then begin to allow yourself to enjoy it. Feel the sun on your face and slowly breathe the fresh air. We are beings of energy. It is you who sees. Our natural state of being is joy and love. Beautiful.

The spiritual journey is one of constant transformation. To grow, you must give up the struggle to remain the same. Learn to always embrace change. In a very deep sense, you free yourself by finding yourself. You are not the pain, stress, or anxiety you feel. You are the one who notices these things. The subject sees the object (the object being a past painful experience). Your way out is to notice who's noticing. It's much less complex than all we do to protect ourselves. The one who notices is already free. Allow these negative energies to pass through. Give the past's painful experiences the space it needs to pass through. Witness it, and then it will go. Then something else will come up. Enjoy all of it. Sit comfortably inside your awareness. Your thoughts are not your awareness. Thought is the recycling of data that we have already processed. Your awareness is your soul. Your awareness is the real you.

Success is being content, peaceful, and kind no matter what life throws at you. Success is remaining completely untouched even while involved in the potentially frustrating activities of life. Why do we want to be something other than who we already are? Or rather be somewhere else? Why do we always feel a boundary? Pain is a protective mechanism that exists so we can preserve the body.

Do not attach significance to thought or emotion. It is of no consequence. Consciousness is beyond memory. There are several types of memory: evolutionary memory, biological memory, experiential memory, DNA memory, schooling memory, social memory, physiological memory, neurological memory. Memory is the basis of boundaries, and consciousness is beyond memory. Grasp life as it is. Then you will do only what is needed. There is a space between you and your body, between you and your thoughts and emotions. Disengage with the physical form. Disengage with memory. Then there is no past and future. All we have is right now.

Clearly realize what is you and what is not you. Realize the difference between the real you (which is your consciousness, your focus, your awareness) and what you have accumulated over your life (your body and mind). We can see clearly only with some distance. Create a space between you and all you've accumulated. Identify with the universe as an infinite identity, a limitless identity. Become interested in the process, not the goal. With spirituality, don't look for an object as in finding God or finding the truth. It is not the object of your search that is important. It is the action of looking.

Life itself and the source of life is the ultimate intelligence. Life does not end with survival. Life begins with survival. Our physical existence is possible only because of our bodies' seamless ability to respond to the entire universe. For example, we inhale what trees exhale. Your identity and intellect are like a sharp knife. A knife is not dangerous in a surgeon's hand, but it is dangerous in a child's hand. The identity of the knife makes it a necessary tool or a dangerous weapon.

Try to choose one quality and become loyal to it. Choose to be peaceful. This will create stillness within you. Skip the emotional roller coaster and head straight to finding the solutions with no sense of insecurity or incompleteness. The people in your life and in your outer world will never be 100 percent the way you want it. But your inner life could always be 100 percent the way you want it. Take responsibility of the experience of your life. The more you are able to respond to everything around you, the freer you become.

Responsibility offers you a choice of action. All an animal must do is eat well. Human beings must do much more than eat well to be successful. Your ability to respond responsibly can play a big part in your success. Responsibility is about being present. Life is a moment-to-moment dialogue with the universe. Responsibility equals "response-ability." And your ability to respond is limitless. The ability to respond is the basis of life. To be loving is a willingness to respond freely and openly. Your ability to love is based on your ability to include. Love is a way of being. You are only using the other person as a key to open what is already within you. Your joy must be on self-start. If I am willing, I can respond to anything.

I am the maker of my life. I am 100 percent *response-able* for everything I am and everything I am not. Responsibility is the simplest and easiest way for you to express your own divinity. Limited responsibility is a way of drawing boundaries for yourself. Become a willing life in this universe. No boundary equals no burden. When you become willing, you become one with the cosmos. This is coming home. Our evolution has gone from a single-celled organism to a human being. This evolution has taken us millions of years, but here we are.

My thoughts are not to be viewed as a nuisance. My ego and thoughts appear to protect me. Even though it may not seem like it, the mind is always trying to protect the body. The mind is not the enemy. It's only trying to help or fix the past and future. It's trying to create the perfect future and trying to fix the imperfections of the past. I am not my thoughts. I am vast. I am extensive. Just as the waves belong to the ocean, my thoughts and emotions are mine. But they are not the real me. The mind thinks just as the heart beats. I am the space that allows the thoughts to appear. Just as the room is the space that allows the table and chairs to exist, I am the space that allows my body to exist. I am many things. I am love. I am acceptance. I am creative. I am intelligence.

So begin exactly where you are. True healing begins with saying yes and accepting this moment. Even if it's filled with doubt, frustration, confusion, or a sinking feeling in your stomach. Do not skip over this moment. Do not reject or run away from this moment. You will be pushing away the intelligence of this moment. All intelligence of life itself is contained within this moment, even if this moment contains despair. We are taught and conditioned not to feel sad or confused. But this confusion is not a mistake. It contains intelligence. The mind is tricky. The mind screams, "Give me wisdom now!" The mind is a seeker and tells us that the next moment will be better. Somehow, the mind does not trust this moment. The mind plays tricks on us because we can say, "I accept this confusion." But only because we want the confusion to go away.

But we can't just state that "I accept this moment." Acceptance does not come from what we say; acceptance comes from what we do. Acceptance occurs when there is no rejection in your perception. Acceptance occurs when you can allow the entirety of this moment to flow through you without holding anything inside. The ocean has already accepted its waves. Every thought and emotion is like a wave, appearing then disappearing then reappearing again. Start to notice what is actually happening right here and now. We look to the future in anticipation of a better life and remember the past to relive the good times. But the real magic is happening right now.

Let the first hour of your day set the theme of success and positivity that will echo throughout your entire day. Today will never happen again. Don't waste it with a false start or no start at all. You are not here to fail. You are here to succeed. Happiness involves enjoying the present moment without anxious dependence upon future hopes and without wishing you were somewhere else. Become satisfied with what you have. When you experience true happiness, you will want nothing more than exactly what you have right now. You will achieve your grand dream one day at a time, one choice at a time.

Set goals for each day. Complete short simple chores that will take you one step closer to your pot of gold. You cannot build your house in one day, so please be patient with yourself. Do the best you can, but enjoy the day and rest satisfied with what you have accomplished. Success is a journey. Today, just like all the others, is a special gift from God. Allow some of your goals to give you joy, a smile, and peace. Plan those daily goals so that they are steps along the path toward those great dreams you secretly hold in your heart. Give yourself every chance to succeed, and if you fail, fail trying. The only true failure is giving up completely.

Search for the seed of good within every adventure. Master that principle, and you develop a precious shield that will guard you well through the darkest alleys you must walk through. Even through the worst of times, there is always a seed of good. We always learn more from our failures than we do from our successes. The real test in life is not in keeping out of the rough times but in getting out after we have messed up. It's not about how hard you can hit, it's about how hard you can get hit, get back up, then keep moving forward. Championships are won by those who have learned to cope with adversity.

Do not take yourself too seriously. Happiness is a by-product of how you treat your fellow man and of how you treat yourself. Share your uplifting message with others. Your future is up to you. Your quality of life will not change much for the better unless you are determined to pay the price with time and effort, sacrifice, and pain. The choice is yours and yours alone. The best is yet to come, providing you play by the rules of life. Use the keys to unlock and open those closed doors in your way. Persevere until you attain your desires. Often, you may feel alone and misunderstood. But you will know a certain freedom that no one else does: the freedom of chasing your dreams with the intention of turning them into your reality. Allow life to unfold for you. The key to all you could accomplish in this lifetime hinges upon your willingness to embrace all that you are for the chance that you may come to experience all that you truly are.

Know that you create your perception. Break the obsession with the illusion of yourself. See yourself in others. You resemble all life-forms in the universe, and they resemble you. The ego can become your enemy if it goes unchecked and convinces you that it is you. If we let the ego lead the way, we become approval junkies in constant need of the approval of our own ego and, of course, of others. If I am not my thoughts, then who am I? What am I? I am the soul, the awareness that watches these thoughts. I am the space that allows these thoughts to appear.

As human beings, we have a primal desire to grow and advance. We are always looking for a bigger and better home, a bigger and better office space or workspace. We have a desire to become infinite. I must remind myself to slow down and take a breath. Everything's going to be okay, even in death. The work you do is a form of prayer. Thinking only complicates things. Do not try to control your mind. It's only an antenna picking up data and memory. The mind is very sharp. You must hold it right or it will cut you.

Whatever you resist becomes the biggest challenge in your life. Consciousness is an intelligence beyond the psychological and physical structure. There is my mind and your mind. My body and your body. But there is no such thing as my life and your life. We all exist within the same life, within the same lifetime. This is a living cosmos, and you have captured some of this life-creating energy. Depending on how much you capture, this will determine the scale of your life. The growth of your body is a result from the food that you've gathered over time. What was soil became food; what was food became your flesh and blood. Whatever you have accumulated cannot be you. It can be yours, but it is not you. Your thoughts are accumulations of impressions that you have absorbed. Your personality has been developed over time and inherited from each person you have encountered and each relationship you have had during your lifetime.

Our two basic faculties are the power of will (body) and the power of thought (mind). We are mostly identified with these two faculties. Consciousness is a dimension of intelligence that is neither the body nor the mind but is the source of both. If you begin to touch this dimension of intelligence, you will naturally begin to identify with it. Walls of self-preservation end up being walls of imprisonment. We want to expand boundlessly, but we cannot become boundless through physical means. Physicality means that there is a defined boundary. There is something within us that is longing to become boundless. Unless we become free of identification with our own physical form, it will be difficult to find freedom.

Do not attach much significance to the mind because the entire body has a mind of its own. Thought is a combination of memory and imagination and what you can create from memory. Data that you have already gathered also appear as thoughts. Your body's memory is a million times more complex than your mind's memory. Your body remembers skin tone and facial features of your ancestors. There is more complicated activity happening in the body than there is in the mind. Your body is a body of intelligence. The very source of creation exists within you right now.

Do not identify with what you accumulate; identify with the source of creation. Identify with the source of what and who you are, which is consciousness, awareness, existence. Identify with the consciousness of all existence. Being peaceful is a fundamental necessity, and one drop of spirituality goes a long way. Once you find a little gap, a little distance between you and your body, between you and your mind….this is the beginning of the end of suffering. Human suffering only happens on the psychological and physical levels. We have not explored the full dimension of who we are because of the fear of this suffering. Our concern is always "What will happen to me if I stop avoiding and face my fears?"

Here is where we must practice: total acceptance and forgiveness. We must believe that whatever happens to us, we will be okay. To survive on this planet, you do not need any divine help; but being prayerful is a fantastic way to keep in conscious contact with the Creator. When we live our lives willingly, it is like heaven. When we live our lives unwillingly, it is like hell. Within every person is a little good and a little bad, a little selflessness and a little selfishness. It is possible to become so willing that your will disappears. Your outside environment and situations will never be 100 percent the way you want it. But you must strive to make what is happening within you 100 percent your way.

Be loyal to your desired qualities. Be loyal to being peaceful and joyful. A special quality of attention is needed to recognize consciousness. God is life; life is consciousness. These are not separate things. We know that we are alive because we are conscious. Don't you agree? We know life and our environment through our five senses. Comparison of what we remember to what we are presently experiencing is only good enough for survival. But as modern human beings, we are looking for and in need of much more than just survival. The brain has been created from within. Our bodies and everything in it have been created from the food we eat. Consciousness is the basis of all physical existence.

Empty space makes up 99 percent of an atom. This proportion is the same in our universe. You can only see your hand because it stops light. If light passed through your hand, you wouldn't be able to see it. Being spiritual means that you have expanded your experience of life past the physical and psychological process. Physicality, what we can see, is defined by a boundary. No boundary equals no burden. Responsibility equals your ability to respond. And your ability to respond is limitless. Limitless equals no boundary, which equals to no burden.

There are five senses to the human being and five elements to the earth: sight, touch, taste, hearing, smell and water, fire, air, earth, space (consciousness). The mind is not located only in the brain. Every cell in the body caries its own intelligence. The physical body equals accumulation of food. The mental body equals accumulation of impressions. They are the hardware and software of your existence and need a quality source of power.

The third dimension of the self is the energy body. If you bring balance to the energy body, you experience balance within the body and the mind. It's like a light bulb. With the right quality of electricity, the light bulb will shine bright. Every human being is a unique combination of the same ingredients. All of existence is made of this same magical energy and ingredients. Every human being is a part of existence, which means we all contain this magical energy within us. Otherwise, we would not be here breathing it.

The source of our lives is the same source of every other lifeform and the source of all creation. This dimension of intelligence, or consciousness, exists in every one of us. Life is the creation, but the source of life is the Creator. In every creature, every plant, every seed, this Creator of life is at work. There are two basic forces within us. The first is the instinct of self-preservation, which compels us to go to great lengths to protect ourselves. The second is the constant desire to expand and to become boundless. We are constantly pushed and pulled between these two longings: the longing to preserve and the longing to expand.

The foundation of the spiritual process is to journey from the boundary-based individual body to the boundless source of creation. We are not struggling with creation's unwillingness to open the doors for us into the beyond; we are struggling with the walls of resistance that we have built around ourselves. This resistance is the most crucial thing to be attended to and broken down. The human predicament can be described as follows: the very seat of our experience is from within, but our perception is entirely outward bound. It is our quality of perception that determines how effective and successful we are and how much we can accomplish in this lifetime. Enhancing your perception means enhancing your ability to receive life just as it is. The moment we begin to fear suffering is when we begin to suffer.

When looking at the entirety of our life, we must believe that everything will be okay, no matter what happens. For every different level of consciousness, or psychological state of mind, our bodies naturally assume certain postures. Conversely, if we consciously get our body into different postures, we can elevate our consciousness. The way we hold our body determines almost everything about us. The body will never lie. All physical creation is a perfection of geometry. Our bodies came from the earth. We take this body from the earth and give it back to the earth when we die.

The sun is the source of life for our planet. Essentially, everything is solar powered. Earth is at the perfect distance for us to benefit from the sun's power. There is an element of the sun in everything that we consume and breathe. Everything from the microscopic to the cosmic level is cyclical. The moon operates on a cycle. The sun operates on a cycle. The planets all have their own unique cycles. All life obeys their own individual life cycle in coordination with the cycles of the sun, earth, and planets, including us.

Maintain your body in such a way that it is no longer looking to avoid or escape life. Maintain it in such a way that it is longing to come alive. If you have not discovered the passion of the life-giving breath that is in every moment of our lives, how can you begin to know any other kind of passion? Only with the heart can one see righteously. What is essential is invisible to our eyes. Death is not the end of our life; it is simply the end of our body.

If you can be conscious of the space between you and your body/mind, you can open a dimension of limitless possibility. Finding this space is the beginning of the end of the fear of suffering. This borderless unity is an experience. It is not a theory, philosophy, or concept. You are not just a woman or a man; you are everywhere. You are everything, and everything is one. Begin to distinguish the difference between what is real and what is illusion. Begin to realize what everything is made from. What appears to be a wooden table and chair is really made of vibrating atoms and molecules originally cut from an oak tree. Are we here to experience life or to think about it?

Laughter comes from the heart. The intellect doesn't want to laugh; it only wants to dissect. Our thoughts will never be bigger than life. Be a witness to your own intellect. Once you realize when logic should be used and when it's necessary to go beyond it, your life will become beautiful. Our individuality is only our idea about ourselves. The intellect is sharp like a knife. Its function is to slice through reality and enable you to determine one thing from another. The hand that holds the knife of the intellect is identity. Your identity manages and determines your intellect. If it is not needed, the mind should remain empty. Spiritual identity equals a living experience.

The intellect stands between you and your experience with the oneness of life. Personalities form from all the people and situations you have encountered, which then become part of the recycled data of thoughts. The information our mind receives daily enters only through our five senses. And we usually perceive things only in comparison. The intellect can be sharpened if you allow it to soak in your awareness. Make the intellect truly discriminatory in the ultimate sense by learning to discern the real from the illusions, from what is existentially true to what is psychologically true.

Awareness is not what you do; awareness is what you are. Awareness is the deepest dimension of the mind that connects us with the very basis of creation. Being blissful becomes natural when accessing awareness. Being awake, sleeping, and death are all just different levels of awareness. Becoming more aware is a process of inclusiveness, a way of embracing this entire existence.

The reason why success may come easily and naturally for one person is that this one person has organized his/her mind to think the way he/she wants. A well-established mind can become a wishing tree. Once your thoughts are organized, your emotions become organized. Thoughts and emotions are separate but connected at the same time. The way we think affects the way we feel. And the way we feel affects the way we think. Both activities happen in the mind. Thoughts usually change much faster than emotions, and it is mostly our thoughts that leads our emotions.

Our endless nature of desire as humans is an expression of longing for infinite life beyond physical existence. Infinity and zero are only positive and negative expressions of the same reality. Enlightenment involves dropping dualities such as like and dislike and attachment and aversion. The sole aim of every individual's life energy is to touch the very source of our making. Quality of life is determined by how we experience life, not by what life offers us.

The universe owes its existence because of the transformation from chaos to order. As human beings, we have inherited this same task of transforming the chaos in our lives into order. As above, so below. Electrons orbit the nucleus just as the earth orbits the sun. The four basic forces in the universe are electromagnetism, strong and weak nuclear forces, and gravity. Electromagnetism is the force responsible for light, magnetism, and electricity. Strong and weak nuclear forces are the two forces that hold atoms together. Supernova explosions that occurred billions of years ago are responsible for forming all the heavy elements in existence such as calcium, phosphorus, iron, cobalt, and nickel.

Atoms from these elements first circulated as interstellar dust. Gravity caused them to clump together to form the planets of our galaxy and solar system. Did the carbon, hydrogen, oxygen, nitrogen, iron, calcium, phosphorus, and sulfur in human beings become conscious and learn to think? They seem to have a mind of their own. Were these elements always conscious? When observing a single cell in the human body, you can see chemical reactions swirling in, out, and through the cell. What you can't see is that these reactions do two things at the same time. They keep the individual cell alive at the local level, and at the holistic level, they keep the entire body alive. As above, so below.

We are the descendants of exploding stars. It took us fourteen billion years to get here. Our bodies and minds contain fourteen billion years of memory, evolution, and transformations. I do not have to think. My spirit just knows what to do. Thinking is secondary. Thinking is a tool to be used, on command, to make important decisions. The need to make an important decision comes along very rarely. My spirit just knows what to do. True freedom is found by diving fearlessly into the hidden depths of the present moment's experience.

The world we see is nothing more than our projection of it. Find deep acceptance of your worst fears, your pain, your sadness, your deepest unfulfilled desires. You must be willing to face them all head-on. When you start to understand how suffering manifests in you, you start to understand how it manifests in everyone else. We are all the same in the most basic ways. We all experience some level of suffering, and we all seek a way out of that suffering. Division is the root cause of all suffering and conflict in life. If my partner were to leave me, I would become anyone who has ever lost someone they love. In the depths of the intimately personal and intensely painful experiences, I discover the impersonal truth of existence, and there, I am free.

We are all pressed down by the weight of our lives, the weight of our history and of our imagined futures. We all walk around with beliefs and stories about ourselves. We all try to make our lives go the way we want them to go, and on some level, we are failing to become who we are not. By focusing on who we are not and what we don't have, we separate ourselves from God and from life in its entirety. We assume that reality is broken and needs to be fixed and that each of us is separate from life. Freedom is all about waking up from the dream that we are somehow separate from this present moment. Embrace all that appears in the vastness that is this present experience. Accept this present experience deeply, and let go of all ideas of how this moment should or should not be. Discover the deep acceptance inherent in every thought, in every feeling, and suffering will come crashing down.

We also have basic longings that urge us to move, to help, to change things, and to make a difference—to be recognized for our actions and sometimes for our beliefs. We are just as much a part of life as the sun. We are life itself, not separate. This realization is only the beginning. We are not broken. We have always been whole and complete. We share an inherent oneness with all of life.

Rooted in oneness, we are free to fully engage with the dance of apparent separation. True healing begins when we get out of the way and accept things as they are and live life fearlessly. Fixating on a destination misses the importance of the journey, which is where life and love truly exist. We are trying to get somewhere else when right here and now is where all of life is. We are all just trying to get home, but in reality, we are already home.

You are the wide-open space in which all thoughts, sensations, sounds, and feelings are allowed to appear and disappear. You are also inseparable from those thoughts, sensations, sounds, and feelings. You are not your thoughts, but at the same time, all thoughts are allowed to come and go in the intimate space that you are. You are not sounds, yet all sounds are allowed to appear and disappear in you. You are the consciousness that holds the vibrations of form. You are the vast and expanding awareness in which the world appears and disappears. At your deepest core, there is silence, wisdom, and knowing. Creativity seems to come out of nowhere within you, then it is expressed through you. Perhaps we are channels that the creativity of the universe flows through.

CHAPTER 26

IDENTITY AND CHARACTER

Just about everything built by humans is inspired by God's design of humans. Highways and streets are like our veins. Vehicles travel up and down streets just like our red and white blood cells travel through our veins and arteries. Our electronic devices and phones are made with the inspiration of our circulatory system. Electrical panels and circuit boards are very similar to our electrical circulatory system in our brain and throughout our entire body.

Our bodies have been made from planet Earth. Planet Earth is just one piece of the universe. We are one piece of planet Earth. As above, so below. The pathways in our brain and lungs look just like tall oak trees. A connecting system of synapses in the brain and bronchi in the lungs resemble tree trunks, branches, and leaves.

There are five fundamental elements, and all five are the building blocks of what we are made from. We would surely die if we were deprived of just one of these elements. Our blood flows through our veins like lava runs through the center of the earth and up volcanos. There is a steady electric current that runs through our body at all times. When the brain commands the body to move, the electric current sent by the brain travels through us faster than lighting bolting down from the clouds. Our thunder is our voice (fire).

We all breathe the same air. We are constantly breathing in oxygen and exhaling carbon dioxide. This is the opposite of what trees are doing. Trees breathe in carbon dioxide and exhale oxygen.

We depend on the trees, and the trees depend on us. This constant exchange of air deeply connects us with the life-sustaining trees. The earth takes one long inhale during fall and winter then one long exhale during spring and summer (air).

When scientists look for life on other planets, the first thing they look for is water. The first form of life on earth was a single-celled organism born in water. From there it evolved into a fish. The fish then evolved to walking on land and breathing air. I have come to believe that this first land walker, over the course of millions of years, evolved into human beings and all other animals that live on land and in the air. Water covers about 70 percent of the earth, and we are made up of about 70 percent water. We must drink water to stay alive and healthy. There is a simple answer to the question, Where did we come from? We came from water (water).

We all stand on the same ground. We eat the fruits and vegetables that grow from the earth. All living things, plants, and animals have been born from Mother Earth. We came from the earth, and our bodies go back into the earth when we pass on (earth). Are you starting to see our significant connection and similarities with our planet? The minerals that created the mountains are the same minerals that created our bodies.

What's holding all these elements together? Just as we are the vast space of awareness where all thoughts and emotions appear and disappear, just as we are the infinite consciousness that allows all contents to exist, God is the fifth element that allows all the elements of our planet and the universe to exist. As above, so below. Just as there are five fundamental elements of our planet, human beings have five senses: taste, touch, sight, smell, and hearing. Without God, nothing else would exist. Simply defined, I understand God to be a power greater than myself. I know that I cannot hold up the sun. Nor can any human. This is just one example of God's will, of God's power and intelligence. As humans, we cannot fully comprehend the power and intelligence of God. The best we can do is give examples, speak in metaphors, and compare God to what it is or what it is not. God's will can be found within the power of gravity. God's will can be found throughout the infinite universe and our spectacular solar system.

Is there nothing holding up the sun in space? This question of holding the sun in space would arise if you think that the sun is fixed at one place in space, but it's not. It's hurtling through space at a speed of around 72,000 kilometers per hour and dragging our solar system with it. It's like throwing a stone into the air. While the stone is traveling through the air, nothing is holding it in the atmosphere; but it is moving. It will continue to move until it slows down because of air friction and then fall back down toward the ground because of the forces of gravity. The example of throwing a stone can be imagined on the cosmic level. The sun is a big fireball moving through space at an incredible speed with no friction to slow it down. The sun orbits the center of our galaxy via gravity. The sun's enormous mass is held together by gravitational attraction, producing immense pressure and temperature at its core.

The oldest stars in our galaxy are nearly as old as the universe itself. It is estimated to contain 100 to 400 billion stars and at least that number of planets. Stars and gases at our galactic center orbit at approximately 220 kilometers per second. This constant rotation speed suggests that about 90 percent of the mass of our galaxy is invisible to telescopes, neither emitting nor absorbing electromagnetic radiation. This invisible mass has been termed *dark matter*. Just because we can't see it doesn't mean it's not there. This is the same proportion to the mass of an atom or to the mass of one cell in our body in that they appear to be 90 percent empty. Just because they seem to consist of mostly empty space doesn't mean that the empty space is made of nothing. As above, so below.

The center of the galaxy contradicts our laws of physics. In other words, we don't fully understand what it is or what it is made out of. There is an intelligence at work here that is much greater and beyond the comprehension of human beings. The center of our galaxy is another example of what I consider to be God. The empty space of the universe and in cells and atoms is where I believe God exists. If God is everywhere, that means that God exists within us as well.

Fundamentally, we are all connected to the same universal intelligence. The same intelligence that holds up the sun. In space, an object in uniform motion will remain in uniform motion unless acted upon by an external force. The moon is orbiting the earth, the earth is orbiting the sun, the sun is orbiting the center of the galaxy, the electron orbits the nucleus, and each one of us is a world of their own.

There are three types of questions: the question is asked just because you are looking for attention; the question is asked about something you have experience with but are looking for confirmation or a second opinion; the question is asked because you truly are looking for the answer. A good leader knows when it's time to follow. Learn, practice, teach…repeat. The leader doesn't set out to lead. He/she is called upon to lead and accepts the responsibility every day.

Okay, so you made some mistakes, experienced some setbacks. You wish you could go back to a better time, a happier time, a better age. Instead of wishing you could go back to the good old days, become better than you used to be. Become better than the best version of yourself you can remember. Because there is no going backward. We must go forward because standing still is not an option. Remember your passions as a young adult? What's stopping you from picking those back up? Go ahead and bring back those hobbies, those arts and crafts, the photography, the painting, the dancing, the singing. Bring it back into your life today. Do it now. Don't look back.

Where to start? Start with repairing relationships. You only get one family, so call your parents and tell them you love them. Call your brothers and sisters just to see how they're doing. Call your aunts and uncles and make plans to hang out just for the sake of spending time with them. You only get one family. We're all very busy, but we must make time for family. Any amount of time spent together will be worth it. You just have to do it. Family gives me strength in numbers. Family makes me feel like I belong. Family recharges my well-being. Family provides a collective group conscious of love that you will not find anywhere else. Yes, we argue and debate over politics, lifestyle choices, and religious beliefs; but after the yelling is over and the smoke has settled, we go right back to honoring one another.

Typical Complaints and Self-Caused Suffering

Walking up early for work. Aren't you lucky to have a job in the first place? Don't you remember how excited you were when you heard that they hired you? What would happen if you no longer had a job? The first thing felt would be the stopping of money flowing into your bank account. Without money coming in, money can't go out. Whether we like it or not, this flow of money is the fuel that manages our lives. I guarantee that there is someone out there that wishes they had your job.

Waking up. This was the biggest struggle for me—being ripped from dreamland and suddenly thrown into reality. For years, I was not content with my life. I struggled to find any real sense of happiness. The only time I felt relief was the few seconds after my first hit of cocaine or heroin. Once that first hit wore off, I spent the rest of the day chasing that first high. That's a race that was impossible to win, and I refused to accept that fact. I was living in a deep denial of what the truth was.

I had many problems that I was unwilling to confront, and instead of repairing my problems at the root, I only hid them with a Band-Aid on the surface. Every morning or afternoon I woke up, the reality of how fucked up my life was smacked me in the face. Before I even took a shower, I traveled a borough away to pick up what I considered to be my medicine. The consequences got worse every day.

Then as the weeks went by while living sober, my quality of living improved a little at a time. I no longer see my life as a cursed existence getting closer to death with each passing minute. Now I see my life as a blessing. I never let myself forget how lucky I am to be alive. How lucky I am to be healthy with functioning organs and limbs. I am no longer tormented constantly by a never-ending screaming in my head for *more, more, more.* My mind is quiet and still. My sanity has been restored. Regaining my sanity is enough reason for me to thank God every morning for giving me my life back.

But it doesn't end there. Now that I have been given the gift of sanity, I am responsible for maintaining it. I am responsible for keeping my body and mind healthy and strong to be able to take care of the people closest to me. It still blows my mind that the same people that I asked to help me when I was struggling are now asking me to help them. I never thought that I would see the day when someone would ask me for help.

Paying bills. Another hard fact of life: we have to pay to play in some way, in every arena. Paying bills are not a problem if you are saving more than you spend and not buying things you can't afford. Another lesson I had to learn the hard way: do not apply for credit cards so you can buy more things. Paying later only causes problems later, even though it may seem to fix problems now. A credit card can be used to consolidate debt into a lower-interest loan. We will always have to give back what we borrow. Borrow only if it is necessary. The only bills that are very difficult to escape are rent, insurance, cell phone, and student loan. If you are disciplined enough to save enough money to put a down payment on a house, then eventually, the rent/mortgage payment will go away. So will the student loan. By keeping the total amount of monthly bills to a minimum, you create a greater opportunity to save much more than you spend.

Not having what you want. After a little time of maintaining sobriety, I started to realize things that I had not known for a very long time. Since I no longer had to spend all my money on drugs and alcohol, all that money stayed in my bank account. Even though I didn't receive a salary increase, it was like getting an instant raise. I was not used to having extra money, and my first thought was not to save it. My first thought was *How do I spend it?*

Now that I had extra money to burn, I started shopping for things that I had wanted to get but could never afford it. My obsessions were transferred to clothes. It was nice to have nice things, but there is such a thing as having too many clothes. After my closet was full, there was no need to continue shopping for more. And that's the key word: *more*. The curse of being insatiable still existed within me.

I was no longer buying clothes because what I had was falling apart; I was buying clothes in an attempt to fill the feeling of emptiness within myself. I was in constant search of trying to find completeness through obtaining material things. Just like chasing that first high, this is a race that is impossible to win. No material thing will ever provide a lasting fulfillment. The best way to learn this lesson is to actually go through this experience of trial and error. To know it, you have to feel it. Someone else's words will never sink in; they have to be your own.

But it doesn't end here. The next action is to understand that you already have everything you need. Find satisfaction and contentment with knowing that you have everything you need. Having what you need is all that you should want. But let's be real. We all want more; we all want better. The trick is to become truly satisfied with what you have but also strive to become better. Strive to increase your quality of living. Do it for you but with the intent of sharing it with the people closest to you. Achieving long-term goals and experiencing that well-deserved satisfaction and happiness is best felt when you can share it with the people you love. Live in the present moment but also plan ahead. Life doesn't get easier as time goes on; we get better at life.

Going to social events. When walking into a large family gathering, or any large gathering for that matter, it is polite and respectful to say hello to every single person in that room. If you're like me, you become instantly overwhelmed by this task that is presented before you. There is no wrong way to do this, and there is no wrong time to do this. Our thoughts can be paralyzing. Thoughts like *Who should I approach first? I just made eye contact, should I approach her? I don't want to bother them. I remember him, should I go over there? I don't want to disrupt their conversation. Should I just pick a corner to sit and let people come up to me? Did I get here too late? Oh my god, I can't say hello to everyone, right? Why do I feel so awkward and unsure of what to do? Why won't anyone come up to me? Fuck it, I'm just going to sit right here, and I'll say hello if I cross paths with anyone.*

As we head into our late twenties and early thirties, holidays, engagement parties, weddings, baby showers, funerals, birthdays, gender reveals, brunches, and long commutes to visit family becomes a repetitive cycle. We all have a lot to keep up with in our busy lives, so it is difficult to attend every event. But if you do have the time, please do not hesitate.

I have come to understand that these events are important. Not only for the person who is inviting you but it is also important for you. My late teenage years into my twenties consisted of partying every day, all day. My social circle was big. Now in my midthirties, my social circle has become much smaller. And that's not a bad thing. A typical weekday for me consists of waking up, going to work, coming home, eating dinner with my wife, then going to bed early enough to get enough sleep so I don't feel like shit the next morning. My lifestyle is focused on working and taking care of myself today so I can continue working tomorrow. Then repeat.

There is no more chaotic partying. I'm able to celebrate life on the weekends and continue working on my side projects and hobbies. But I still have to wake up Monday morning, so I really only get one full day to myself each week. I have come to accept this hardworking lifestyle. Because I give 100 percent toward advancement in life and an improved quality of living, I see the results of my hard work. And those results, even though they are slow and steady, are what keep me going. My progress enables me to sleep at night, and it makes we want to get up the next morning and look forward to the day. This may seem like common sense to some, but for me, this is a complete one-eighty from my previous perspective.

Anyway, adult social events are as fun as you want them to be because you have the ability to make them as fun as you want them to be. The point is, don't take these opportunities for granted. These gatherings are our new parties and celebrations of life. It's a chance to get out of the house, have some fun, and make new memories.

I always felt like an outsider because I saw myself as an outsider. If instead, I viewed myself as one of the group, then I could become part of the group. See everyone in the group as equals, including yourself. Everyone is equally important, including yourself. In social environments, you can't pick and choose. You must include everyone as equals. Once you start to pick and choose who the outsider is, then they start to pick and choose who the outsider is. Don't label yourself as an outsider; see yourself as an equal. We are all equally important.

I have beliefs that are so ingrained, so habitual, and such a reflex that I don't even realize they are there. And these ingrained beliefs are controlling and forming my perspectives, thoughts, and emotions. Self-acceptance is an important therapeutic theme. It is largely the self-defeating thoughts and resulting feelings and actions that sabotage our lives. The problem becomes our thinking rather than our drinking and self-destructive behavior. We must change our automatic thoughts and general beliefs of what we tell ourselves about our problems, the difficult emotions we experience in attempting to address our problems, and most important, what we tell ourselves about ourselves.

Discomfort anxiety is the emotion one feels when anticipating pain, discomfort, or unpleasantness. It is brought about by the belief that discomfort is unbearable and that it cannot and must not be tolerated even for one minute. Even though it may feel like you're going to die from your own mental insanity, you will not. First, recognize what is actually happening in those moments. Determine and recognize what is causing the unpleasantness and the discomfort. My discomfort is usually brought about by my wanting to be somewhere else, doing something other than what I am doing. My focus is on the future, completely denying my present situation and environment. I am anticipating the pain of being somewhere I don't want to be, and by anticipating the pain, I cause inner pain and suffering.

Before the anxiety completely takes over, I take a long breath, observe my current situation, and without judging or labeling anything, I allow everything I am experiencing through my five senses to flow through me. I stop labeling what is favorable and what is unfavorable. I stop rejecting everything I am seeing, hearing, and feeling. Instead of wishing I was somewhere else, I thank God for bringing me to this moment. Then I remember how lucky I am to be here, how lucky I am to be healthy, and how lucky I am to be alive.

If selfish thoughts and negative feelings start to arise, they are most likely coming from the selfish parts of my ego. Then I realize who I am there for. I take the focus off my own selfish wants and put it toward the people who are important to me. If I keep my focus on what I want for too long, I begin to suffer. Because my outer world will never be 100 percent the way I want it, I have to accept that. But I do have more control of my inner world. In some ways, it is our own doubts and insecurities that stand in the way of our peace and happiness. With heaven's help, I cast my demons out!

Keep pushing for the thing that you want, but manage your expectations. We never know what life will throw at us next. But we have two choices: run from it or run toward it. Face the fear. Accept the situation. The current situation could be a consequence of a past action. Go with the grain instead of going against it.

I have problems with impulse control and with conforming to authority. I have a compulsion to run from my current reality. I am too quick to react to my thoughts and urges. Although it is difficult to do, I practice waiting five to ten minutes until the urge goes away and a new thought arises. Common sense usually kicks in around then, and I'm able to make a more practical and mature decision.

There are many different compartments to my personality. There is a part of me who only wants to do what's right and is optimistic about the future. That part of me doesn't want to do anything to disrupt my bright future. The devilish side of me is the selfish and compulsive side and only wants to take everything I can get my hands on before I lose the opportunity. The experienced side of me weighs the options and remembers the lessons of the past and from there can predict the future. I always know what the right thing is to do. I just don't listen to my conscience and try to get away with selfish actions.

Are you looking for yourself in a million different ways? When we fall in love, our search for love falls away. The seeker didn't find love; the seeker disappeared. The illusion of you and me falls away, and we become one. That is love. The illusion of separation falls, and what is left is unity. What we really long for is a deep intimacy with our own experience of life, with every thought, sensation, and feeling. What we are really looking for, on the deepest level, is ourselves. Not the ego-made illusion thought story you tell yourself, but yourself as the wide-open space that holds all life. Yourself as in your true self, who you are beyond the illusion, behind the story. What you seek is what you already are.

Not seeing this, we go out into the world and seek that completeness in another person or in other activities. You are the vast awareness that allows everything to be. Only allow positivity. It is our responsibility to eliminate all negativity at the root to keep our harmony pure within. We are the creators of good and the destroyers of evil, the keeper of our own destiny. The devil preys upon those weak of faith. Build your spiritual foundation upon solid concrete, rooted deep within the earth. A man/woman that wants nothing is invincible.

Find your wavelength. It's tied to your breath, heartbeat, and emotion. When going through anxiety, our breath is heavy and our heartbeat is fast. This produces a volatile wavelength. When we are going through depression, our breath is shallow and our heartbeat is weak. This produces a wavelength that hovers just above the zero line on the x-axis. When we become peaceful and harmonious with our environment, our breath is strong and consistent. Our heartbeat is strong and steady. This is our most natural state of being. This allows our wavelength of energy to be rock steady and consistent.

Outside forces, situations, and people will throw off your wavelength from being peaceful to disturbed then sometimes into anger if you are pushed hard enough. Recognize when this happens. Accept the situation or person for what or who they are. Accept your inability to change them at the moment. But also understand that you do have the ability to control what is happening within you. Regain your wavelength. Regain your inner peace. Regain your confidence and style. Stabilize yourself internally. Find your natural wavelength of energy.

Everyone's wavelength is a little different. Our energy wavelengths are like musical notes. Some are compatible with others and create harmony. Some clash and just do not sound right when played together. Learn what your wavelength of energy is. Recognize what it feels like, and stay loyal to it. Outside forces will disturb your flow, your wavelength. An important practice is learning how to regain your wavelength and learning how to regain it quickly.

Our posture and how we hold ourselves upright determines every aspect of our being. Our posture speaks directly to what's going on within us. Our thoughts and emotions reflect through and directly affect our posture. Breathe in from your belly, not the chest. Stop suppressing emotions into the stomach, and allow only free-flowing air to pass through your entire body. When we deprive ourselves of free-flowing air, thoughts, and emotions, we become no more advanced than a soldier at war. We live, we fight, and die and nothing more.

Only humans understand the value of emotion. We can and often communicate through them. We can communicate with each other without saying a word because we understand the language of emotion. Emotion is the poetry of expression. Everything is connected to everything within our body, our mind, our soul, and our universe. And the way we hold ourselves tells the story of what we are going through at that moment. Become aware of your posture. By changing your posture, you can change your mood. When standing or sitting, hold your spine straight. Tuck your hips in. Keep your shoulders back and square but relaxed. Breathe in from your diaphragm. Take a long breath in and release a long breath out. From this posture, you will be able to find strength and confidence more easily.

Gravity is constantly pulling us down. To live through the day with strength, we must keep our posture straight. Gravity has the least resistance on us if our weight is dispersed straight down from the head through the spine and straight down to the feet. The body will experience minimal pain if hold ourselves this way. If the posture is lazy with stooped shoulders and a curved back, the weight will be dispersed to many unnecessary places causing pain in the neck, upper and lower back, hips, knees, ankles, and feet. The more we allow gravity to win, the quicker we age.

Our posture also affects the functioning of the mind. The goal is to calm and quiet the mind. Quieting the mind starts with observing the mind with no judgment. No psychoanalysis of yourself. Just be the silent witness of yourself and your environment and nothing more. With practice over some time, changes will begin within you. Your awareness will begin to expand. Now you are not moving the body with your mind and ego as the leader; your awareness becomes the leader. Awareness is the innermost quality of our being. It is our soul. Through true recognition of your soul, your entire being rejoices. Witness your harmony with life as a constant stream of energy and vibration. Become connected with the vibration and energy of all life with the universe as infinity.

Body and mind have a consciousness of its own, and as we become one with it, we naturally become more loving, compassionate, respectful, friendly, and intimate. Society and our jobs demand the attention of our mind. There is no place for heart in business. But if we are able to use both head and heart at the right time, we are indeed ahead of the game. Knowing when to use your head and knowing when to use your heart involves listening to your instinct. It's difficult to explain in words what your instinct sounds like, but when we refer to our instinct, we know where to look for it. This is going with your gut feeling. This is doing what feels right. Our instincts our primal and have been passed down to each one of us as an ancient intelligence. Become familiar with your instincts. They will never lie or deceive you.

Our goal is to go beyond life's duality of opposites. Beyond yes and no. Beyond favorable and unfavorable. Beyond life and death. Good exists because of evil. Beauty exists because of ugliness. Life exists because of death. One cannot exist without the other. For every action, there is an equal and opposite reaction. The real you is beyond duality. Become deeply identified with your spirit, your consciousness. Your head and heart both belong to it. A spiritually conscious person uses their heart as the ruler and their mind as the servant—unidentified with both, only witnessing them.

If we only live our lives within the rules and expectations of our society, our life and our world becomes smaller and smaller.

Working on expanding your awareness and identifying with your soul enhances your life and your existence in many ways. Wisdom consists of not knowing many things but of knowing one thing. That one thing is knowing your awareness and its separation from your body and mind. After some practice, patience, and understanding of this, a day will come when you are in love with all of existence, all of life, and everything in it. You will be able to experience the universe as yourself and yourself as the universe. Practicing this perception is working toward enlightenment. We begin to realize our potential.

Surrender gives clarity where preferences of like and dislike no longer guide our life. Sometimes we find ourselves waiting for some magical moment to happen that will change our lives for the better. But it never comes. The magical moment is the moment we finally follow through with the changes we want to make within ourselves. The moment we actually do what we have been putting off for way too long. The moment we face our fear instead of running from it. That's when magical things start to happen in our life: when we truly follow our heart and make our dreams a reality. Our dreams may seem difficult to achieve, but they are not impossible ideas. They only seem that way when we are running in the opposite direction or when we are not taking the necessary steps we know we should be taking.

The most important step is the first one. The first step is usually the hardest as we tread through unfamiliar territory. But just like everything else, we get better with practice. It might not be confidence that drives us forward; it might be the fear of failing or the fear of mediocrity. It might be the curiosity of wanting to see if we can actually do this and stick with it. Either way, once we get that ball rolling, we don't ever want to see it stop.

So take that first step toward that dream or that goal. Live one day sober. Save one dollar. Apply for that class. Take those lessons. Start writing with one sentence. Pick up that paintbrush and start with one color. Make that phone call. Make that appointment. Ask that question. Take one step toward achieving that dream.

Do not run from fear; allow it to be there. Do not just feel the feeling and then try to hide or deny it. When we deny what we are feeling, we are keeping ourselves separate from the feeling. This is the basic disunity that causes misery. The experiencer is the experience. Don't create the division of subject and object. The goal is to achieve unity with yourself and everything in your environment. A choiceless awareness of what it is, is the key to opening the innermost mystery of your being. Do not label anything as good or bad, favorable or unfavorable. This is how unhealthy attachments and rejections are formed. To survive in today's world, we need to make some form of judgment sometimes. That is what keeps us safe from harm and out of the reach of evil.

Practice keeping a judicial judgment when it's appropriate. Do not separate yourself from this moment. Become one with this moment. The one is only that which arises through our senses and changes from moment to moment. Our acceptance or rejection of what we are experiencing makes no difference in the fact that whatever we are rejecting is still there. In some way or another, rejection causes pain. The more we are able to accept, the lighter we become. Freedom is experienced through way of acceptance. The universe already accepts you. You are already worthy. You have already been accepted by God. So unconditionally accept yourself.

This level of acceptance is the key to your transformation. But it must be true acceptance of not just the good parts but the bad parts too. The universe will always stay in balance with itself, and so must we. We cannot experience happiness without some sadness. We won't know sunshine without the rain. We won't feel pleasure if we never felt pain.

It is so very important to have trust in what you consider to be God, to have trust in the universe, to have trust in yourself. All we have to do is be there on time. Everything else falls into place. I trust that as long as I'm doing the right thing, everything will be okay overall and in the long run. Because bad things will happen. They must happen. We must be able deal with the bad just as we are able to deal with the good. When I step back and look at the entirety of my life, I realize it's really not that bad.

Things could be better? Yes. But things could have also gone a lot worse. It's best to focus on and appreciate what we have right now. We have come a long way. We have learned from our mistakes, and we have grown stronger and wiser because of it. Nothing can take that away. If there is something that you are longing for, you are going to have to put in work to get closer to it. People are attracted to other people not just from looks. We are attracted to each other's energy, character, and aura. Don't give up on your goal and sell yourself short. Don't get in your own way. Trust yourself that if you are doing the right thing, you will eventually get to where you are trying to go. When you put your trust in the universe and in yourself, the universe will guide and support you. The sun will always shine brightest in the direction of your righteous journey.

I will admit that sometimes it is difficult to practice what prophets are preaching. Acceptance and forgiveness are the most freeing actions to take but also can be the most difficult because it happens on such an emotional and subconscious level. You can't just say "I accept this difficult truth." It must be felt and believed on a deep emotional level. It must go from a thought into an ingrained belief. And beliefs are not formed overnight. Beliefs are formed and cultivated through life experiences, consequences, and learning from those consequences, whether good or bad.

Our misery and suffering begin once we start to imagine being somewhere other than where we are right now in the present moment. Once we would rather be somewhere else. Once we would rather be someone else. Once we would rather have something else. Once we start wishing for the past or trying to get to the future in hopes of a better life than what we have right now. Once we start trying to recreate the good old days. This is the moment when misery and suffering begin.

If you feel optimism toward your future, that's different. You are content with where you are but realize that your future will only get brighter from here. Appreciate the present moment, how far you've come, and what you've accomplished. Based on our progress so far, we are able to predict and foresee a successful future. Trust your instincts, trust in yourself, and trust in your choices. The universe works with you when you are doing the right thing. When you're not trying to escape it, when you are respecting yourself and everything around you, the world is beautiful. That's the main takeaway here. Accept, appreciate, and respect the present moment. Don't try to escape it. By trying to escape the present moment, we create misery for ourselves.

You have to get good at catching yourself wishing or trying to escape. You have to be able to recognize and catch negative thoughts early enough where they can't take you over. You must become aware of your ego's voice. Become aware of your subconscious thoughts and engrained beliefs and watch how they form opinions within you about what you are seeing in your outside world. Practice watching yourself and watching out for yourself with the intention of deterring negative thinking.

We all get negative thoughts. We all have that inner voice. Sometimes it's helpful, and sometimes it's just nonsense. Learn the difference between your thoughts and your awareness, your ego and your instinct. Promptly admit when you are wrong, and apologize when it's due. Never lie to yourself. Be as honest as you can with yourself. Denial can cause us to repeat the same mistake over and over.

It's not cool to hate yourself. It's not cool anymore to have the "I don't care" attitude. If you say that you don't care about yourself, it's a defense mechanism as a way of avoiding getting hurt and thus denying yourself happiness. To be happy, you also have to let yourself be vulnerable to being sad and getting hurt. To live a life of true freedom, we must accept everything that life throws at us then deal with it the best way we know how.

Saying you don't care is a way of avoiding responsibility. It's lazy. It's very difficult to love someone that hates themselves. People that don't respect themselves have a lonely existence. If anyone says they're okay with that, I believe that to be a denial that I know very well. The attitude of not caring about anything is a way to protect yourself emotionally if and when anything goes wrong. Dealing with the difficult aspects of life is just as much a part of life as experiencing the good times. A well-balanced person can handle both the good and the bad in a responsible way. Don't say you don't care when you know that you do.

Accept what you cannot change. Realize what you can change. Accept what you cannot do. Understand what you can do. Don't be afraid of getting upset over what you have no control over. It's important to learn and understand the difference between the two. If you notice that you're starting to gain weight and your pants don't fit as well as they used to, don't give up and say you don't care as a way to protect your pride and ego. Take back control and start lifting weights on a regular basis. Eat healthier. If you stay disciplined with a steady workout routine, I guarantee you will see results.

The theme here is don't say you don't care when you really do. We are playing a rigged game called life. Sometimes it seems, from where I'm standing, that the lazy are rewarded and the ambitious are punished. Sometimes it's difficult to find motivation. To get the job, you have to have experience. How will I get experience if I don't get the job? To become popular, you must be known by a lot of people first. To become rich, you first have to have a lot of money. To have a successful business, you will already need to have a successful business.

Start with small short-term goals, small achievements, small easy wins. There will be setbacks because that's just how life goes. No one really admits this, but everyone is behind schedule. Life almost never goes according to plan. Be ready for this so you're not surprised when it happens. Once you start winning a little, you get the ball rolling for winning. Wins become more frequent, bigger as time goes on, and start to outweigh the losses. Winning becomes more normal than losing. When setbacks occur, make sure you pick up where you left off and keep going forward. When setbacks occur, this is moment you must try harder, focus more, pay attention more closely, and give it more energy to get back on track.

Once back on track, you can kick it back into cruise control. The setbacks are the tests. Your ability to overcome them will determine how successful you are in just about everything you do. So yes, we are playing a rigged game. But we must figure out how to start tipping the scales in our favor. One step at a time. One achieved goal at a time. One small win at a time.

There are some things that you have no control over. But there are things that you do have control over. Life is not easy. I don't think it was ever supposed to be. That's why we must get better at life a little more each day. As we get older, life doesn't get easier; it gets harder. We as individuals must get better, wiser, and more skillful at life. Keep a clean house and stay organized. See the world through loving eyes. Surround yourself with people you can learn from. See yourself in other people that are less fortunate than you. Save and invest your money wisely. Keep artistic hobbies in your life as an alternative way to express yourself in tangible ways.

Growth is a slow process. Progress is slow when working toward improving your quality of life. Have patience with yourself, other people, and the universe. Practice makes perfect. Keep doing what you're doing, and you will get there. If you get knocked down, get right back up and keep going! The ability to get back up quickly is what separates the winners from the losers. Trust and believe in yourself, pay attention, and listen closely to your heart. If it feels correct within your heart, then it will be correct within your world.

I believe sadness stems from lack. Sadness is what's left in the absence of happiness. I believe sadness comes from having something taken away or wishing for something that you never had or wanting something you feel you may never have. Happiness stems from fulfillment, feeling complete. Believing that you are exactly where you should be. Believing that you have everything that you need and want. Both sadness and happiness are two feelings of the same coin. We fluctuate between the two. And of course, both are more complex than wanting or not wanting.

But focus more on fulfillment. When I am content or happy, sadness is not there. Or at least, it is very far away. Spirituality goes beyond the emotional feelings of happiness and sadness. Spirituality goes beyond thought and emotion. Our consciousness, our spirit, is like a deep still lake. Thoughts and emotions cause ripples in the lake, and ripples are not necessarily bad. Our spirit contains ancient and divine wisdom. When we reach a state of unity with our body, mind, and universe, there is no internal dialog or debating within ourselves. Only knowing. Only trust. Only acceptance. Without any uncertainty.

Thoughts and emotions constantly push and pull us in opposite directions. Wisdom allows us to be still inside and out. Stop listening to inner voices that tell you that you need something more or different than what you have right now. That's your childish ego at work. Stop listening to inner voices that tell you that you should be somewhere else or that you don't belong here. Again, that's your impatient ego at work. Stop listening to your mind and start listening to your heart. Learn the difference between your thoughts and your awareness. Focus on your ability to focus. Watch yourself watching yourself.

A quiet and still mind is the goal, but you won't experience a quiet mind with one day of practice. It takes time to realize and to reach a place of inner stillness. Spirituality is a way of life; it's a practice. Just like doctors practice medicine, we are always improving our practice with continued education, dedication, discipline, and focus. It's not like learning to type properly on a keyboard because you memorized where all the keys are. Our spirit is infinite and always expanding. Therefore, there is no point where the learning stops. We are ever evolving. We learn a little more each day. We grow a little more each day.

First step to doing anything is becoming willing to try. The next step is to give it a sincere try. If you happen to not do so great, get right back up if you fail or fall. The only true failure is giving up completely. Continue making progress by taking one step in the right direction every day. Try every morning. Try every day. Try every night. Never give up on your faith. Never give up on your trust of the universe. Never give up on yourself. Keep trying until trying becomes second nature, until what used to feel like a struggle becomes an easy pleasure.

CHAPTER 27

THE RELATIONSHIP WITH MY PARENTS

My dad was my Little League football coach. The training I went through at football practice also carries over for the training needed in life: The water is right there on the sideline. You can go take a break and drink some water whenever you want. But I am here to push you. And you are here to push yourself as hard as you can without taking a break then to keep going because you don't get breaks in life. You don't get water breaks in the field. The clock is ticking, and you are expected to perform and do well every day. If you can't handle it, go home. This is survival of the fittest. So you better get good at something. Because no one will do your work for you. If the man next to you is better and faster than you, he will take your place, and you will be sitting on the bench the entire game. Try hard. Practice long. Be patient with the growing process. But you must constantly work on improving your craft, your trade, and your skill. You are like a knife. But you shouldn't be getting dull with use. You should be getting sharper. Now sprint!

My parents still saw me as a little kid well into my thirties and probably still have a hard time seeing me as an adult today. I have heard this to be true for many parents. As their children, I believe it is our responsibility, at the very least, to respect our parents. They have provided us a rent-free home into our late teenage years. Looking back as an adult, I see how valuable that was. Even when we are not getting along or not seeing eye to eye, I still show them respect. I always remember that they did the absolute best they could do. They gave us as much time as they could. They taught us as much as they could. They provided as much as they could. But parents must also take care of themselves. I have held resentments against my parents for being too strict and for not being more like a friend to me. Even though we would fight often, now I can see that they were trying to guide me in such a way that they felt was best.

Let them know that you love them. Call them often. Take the time to visit them. You only have one mother. You only have one father. They are the foundation of our lives. Let them know that they did a good job raising you. Remind them that the kids are supposed to move out. It means the parents did a great job by helping you become self-sufficient and independent.

It seems that parents have a difficult time seeing us as adults. We are forever their babies. I'm sure you've heard this a thousand times: "You'll understand when you have kids of your own" or "You'll understand when you're older." I see how innocent this is coming from the parents' perspective; but parents must also understand that this way of treating us as kids hurts our development as adults, and it hinders our child-to-parent relationship.

We want to be treated as equals when we are growing up. We want to be acknowledged as adults somewhere around sixteen years old. We are maturing fast. We learn a lot because we have all the information of the world at our fingertips. Our phones and the internet are used as a library. Meet us halfway. We will always be your babies, but you must acknowledge our maturity into adulthood. Trust that we will always come back to visit. We will always stay in touch. Maybe not as frequent as you want, but you both will always be a very special part of my life. To my parents, you are still my heroes, and I will always look up to you. I consistently strive to make you proud. You have given me the tools and qualities to succeed in life, and I promise never to waste them.

Until you're in their position, how do you know you could do a better job? Through the struggles and through the ups and downs? But don't be afraid that you will not be a good parent yourself one day. Do not let the fear of failing guide your decisions. Take what you agree with and leave the rest. Do it your way. Do what you think is best. I believe most of our parenting skills come from our primal instincts. Don't doubt yourself. Be the amazing parent you know you can be. Provide all the things that you wish you had and also provide the things that you appreciated, then and now.

Now that I am a parent, I am realizing everything all at once. It is very difficult to reset, unwind, relax, and switch into "off the clock" weekend mode the moment I get home from work. I have a very tough time letting go of the stress, frustration, anger, and confusion the hectic workday brings. I know a lot of people feel the same way. So how would it have been any different for my parents? It wasn't. It was the same thing, the same scenario. The details are slightly different but essentially, it's the same thing. Working during the day then parenting at night is very difficult. There's no doubt about it. Each individual handles it in their own way, the best way they know how. Sometimes we think about what we are going to do, sometimes we ask for advice, but most of the time I think we are just shooting from the hip, going with the flow. I believe listening to your heart, rather than your mind, is the best way to go about it. Be on the lookout for the kid who secludes himself from the family.

There's Something Wrong with That Boy

Talk to him, Dad. I can clearly see that he is unsure of himself and his surroundings. That boy needs guidance. And not just from anyone. That boy needs guidance from you. I see myself as that boy. I was that boy, and in some ways, I am still that boy. He doesn't eat dinner with the family, and you allow this to happen? That is a clear cry for help. He feels like an outsider because he is left out of the family gatherings. Talk to that boy, Dad. Fix it now, before it's too late.

I had a great dad growing up. I still have a great dad now. He taught me the basics of how to walk, how to talk, and how to eat. In doing so, he taught me how to be independent, self-sufficient, and to figure things out on my own. I had to learn how to live as an adult by watching the older men around me. My perspective on life was filled with so much uncertainty growing up. I figured out the complexities of life as I went on. Maybe that was his intention: to make me self-sufficient by letting me figure things out on my own, forcing me to learn as I go on my own without help or direction from anyone.

To his credit, it worked. But I have been lonely. I know loneliness very well. It took me a very long time to become well-adjusted. Within my loneliness, I have hurt myself on the deepest of levels. Talk to that boy, Dad. Before it's too late. Silence equals no guidance. And those who experience long periods of silence will grab at anything just to fill that void. I am in no way pointing a finger or placing blame on anything or anyone. There are many things that we do not have control over.

We must let our kids explore the world and everyone in it, including themselves. Kids are going to get dirty. They are going to get hurt. They will experience pain. We all have fallen down, but the most important lesson to teach is to get back up! Learn from the mistakes. Some of us need to get burned to learn not to touch the flame. That was the only way for me to get through my stubbornness.

As a teenager, I felt invincible. As I got older, my painful experiences cut deeper and deeper. Painful memories dulled the light of my soul, and I became a shell of man. My life was ruled by my addictions, and at that point, I no longer had control over my actions. By the grace of God, my desperation, and my determination to repair myself and my relationships, I have regained my sanity. Thank you, thank you, thank you for never giving up on me! I am forever in your debt. I respect and love you both unconditionally.

The History and Story of Santa Claus

What will you tell your kids? Because they hear it from you first. Then as they get older, they hear things from friends and other asshole kids that Santa isn't real. Then they ask you if Santa is really real. What will you do then? At that point, you have to tell them the real story about Santa or keep lying to them as other kids keep filling their head with doubt. Eventually, you have to come clean and tell them the truth. And when heard for the first time, that truth is a devastating realization.

Why do we keep up this strange tradition of tormenting our children by creating magical moments then taking them away? Why do we make our kids believe that life is filled with mysterious and wonderful characters? Are we preparing them for our theories about God? If we're subconsciously preparing our kids for our theories on God, shouldn't we do a better job of explaining the story of Santa? Why not just tell them the truth from the start? What is the truth? Is Santa real, or is he not real?

My answer to that is Santa is real. Santa Claus was a real man who gave out presents to the kids in his town. We keep the spirit of Santa alive by carrying out his generous work. We become Santa when we leave presents under the Christmas tree and in the personalized stockings, from wherever they're hung. We create the same magic and mystery that Santa once brought to his town when he was alive. The magic that is experienced by every kid on Christmas morning; that is Santa Claus's spirit at work, alive and well. That magic is his legacy. Just like an artist lives forever through their artwork. Just like a musician lives forever through their music. Santa lives forever through us carrying out his legacy of creating magic for our kids on Christmas morning. That is what I will tell my kids when they learn how to speak. No crazy stories. No lying. No making them believe in something then taking it away. No bullshit.

I will tell my kids my version of Santa Claus and that it is now my responsibility to carry out his legacy. Now it's my responsibility to give you magical Christmas mornings you will always remember. And then when my children have kids of their own, it will be their responsibility to carry out the work of Santa. So yes, Santa Claus is real. Santa Claus lives on through us.

Please understand that reaching a place of spiritual oneness and emotional healing will not be reached overnight. The first step is to study and understand the complexities of what you are interested in learning about. The next step is to practice those teachings in your everyday life. These spiritual practices must become part of your daily routines and must become like a reflex similar to blinking. We blink automatically, subconsciously. But we can also control it if we choose.

Our emotions work in a similar way. I still make mistakes. I still fall down. Sometimes my emotions get the best of me, and I still get thoughts that try to convince me that it's okay to go and get a little high. But I practice challenging those negative thoughts. It is very clear to me now that using drugs would be the same as drinking poison. So when negative thoughts appear in my mind telling me to go seek out drugs, out loud I say, "No. That is the worst possible thing I could do right now. Thank you, God, for restoring my sanity."

I've come a long way, but I am far from perfect. The purpose of writing this book is to provide an inside look at my life, my mistakes, my lessons learned, and how I try my best to maintain a healthy and productive life. I have met and heard from plenty of addicts and everyday people to know that my struggles are very similar to your struggles. I feel it is my responsibility to reach out to next suffering individual and share what I have learned in the hopes that the information I am providing will be a guide for you. At the very least, I want to point you in the right direction.

When I least expected it, when I wasn't looking for it, I was sitting outside my apartment smoking a cigarette only a few weeks into my sobriety, and I felt a hand being gently placed on my shoulder. When I turned around to see who it was, no one was there. I realized what happened, and then my eyes welled up with tears. I believe something supernatural touched me to let me know that I am going the right way and that everything is going to be okay. Maybe it was my guardian angel. Maybe it was one of my grandparents standing next to me for a moment. I definitely felt something angelic was watching over me, and I still do throughout my everyday life. This was an event in my life that only further cemented my belief that life and death is much more complex than it seems.

CHAPTER 28

MY WIFE

Melissa and I were married in New York at St. Paul the Apostle Church on December 31, 2020. Before we made it to that day, I went through many changes. As a result, our relationship went through many changes. She saved me from killing myself. She helped to transform me into an adult. She believed in me when I didn't believe in myself and had an amazing amount of patience with me while I went through the most difficult challenges of my life. She made me a father. She provided a sense of security in my life, something I have been very unfamiliar with for a very long time. Because of her, I have an optimistic perspective of my future. She made me stronger and well-adjusted to life. She was a driving force for me to get healthy again. She found me overdosed in the staircase of our apartment building and saw it through to get me back on my feet again. I owe her a never-ending gratitude. Although I may not always show it, I could never forget how she literally and metaphorically saved my life. Melissa, I will always come back home to you. I vow to be a loving husband and providing father. We are perfect for each other, and I love you with all my heart.

You Only Get Upset When You Truly Care

Coming home and turning off work mode has always been difficult for me. My job is emotionally draining and stresses me out often. When I get home, the last thing I want to do is talk about my stress-filled day. All I really want to do is change into comfortable clothes then rest on the couch for a while until my anger and frustration fade away. The problem is as soon as I come home, Melissa wants to talk about everything: her day, her plans, her conversations with her friends, our next vacation, paying bills. I can handle these conversations, but not as soon as I walk through the door.

Somehow, I have to compromise. I have to at least meet her in the middle. I cannot be completely selfish and go hide in my room until I feel like coming out to deal with what she wants to talk about. I find it helpful to remember when we first met. I remember how I felt about her and my desire to meet her. Isn't it funny how the opposite is happening now? I'm avoiding her in the same way she was avoiding me when we first met and started dating. She was chasing me to have a conversation the same way I was chasing her to have a conversation.

Coming home from work is sometimes the moment when my patience is tested. This is where my ability to respond responsibly is tested. Instead of taking an hour or two to unwind after work, I must be able to unwind within five minutes. The first thing I do is ask her for five minutes to shake off my anger. Sometimes it's difficult for me not to take everything personal. Maybe it's a weakness of mine, but when the guys tell me not to take it personal when I get yelled at by the boss, I just can't seem to let it go at first. It takes me a little while to snap back into a still and peaceful mindset.

Ask for five minutes when you get home. Take a few slow breaths and compose yourself. Remember how lucky you are to have the job you have. Remember how lucky you are to have the relationship you have and the family you have. Remember how lucky you are to have the apartment you have. Progress in quality of living is a slow and steady process. Save as much money as you can. Do your own research and start investing your money. Do not live beyond your means. Wake up early for work every day. Be patient with yourself and your progress. Be patient with the one you love.

Melissa, I apologize for all the stress and frustration I have caused. I apologize for the seed of doubt that I have planted in your mind. Thank you for having infinite patience with me. Thank you for your never-ending belief in me. Please allow every day I come back home to you to be a reminder that I promise to continue to do the right thing. I have vowed to make my living amends by continuing to better myself with the intentions of being a great provider and a leader for the family.

Chapter 29

The Difference Between Belief and Knowing

I have reached a point in my psyche, in my being, where I can say that I know who I am. I know where I came from, I know where I'm at, and I have a good idea where to go from here. My inner-world beliefs match what I am seeing in my outer world. For the first time in my life, I actually feel like an adult. I was never able to say that, only up until recently. Once I was able to remove the drugs and alcohol, I was able to watch myself mature.

Without inner demons holding me back, I can truly move forward in life. For about fifteen years, it felt like I was going in circles. I have been on a fifteen-year long downward spiral into my own personal hell. It's a proud moment for me to recognize that I have broken free of my self-inflicted chains. I know I must be careful not to become overconfident. I can't say I got it because an addict never has it.

After some time of living sober, it may seem as if I am cured of my disease. But that is the insidiousness. The disease of alcoholism is so cunning it makes the inflicted believe that it is truly gone after some sobriety time. In turn, the alcoholic now thinks he can drink safely again. Once the first drink is taken, the monster is woken up. Craving and fiending kick in again. Cravings and the obsession with getting the next drink or drug are near impossible to stop. We must continually work on our sobriety, which includes improving our relationship with God, our relationship with all people close to us, and our understanding of ourselves. When you understand why you did what you did, you understand why other people did the same. We can relate to each other because we know what it feels like to go through hell. With this newfound wisdom, our responsibility has now become to teach what we have learned and to reach out to the next suffering individual that comes across our path.

Drugs and alcohol were never my root problem. Yes, I abused and became addicted, but my real problem lies within my being and my personality, with my thoughts and emotions, which I never had control of or, more importantly, an understanding of. I never understood where I came from. I never understood my purpose. I never understood the reason why I was alive. I never understood my own existence.

From the beginning, it was always a guessing game for me with every move I made. I have been through more pain and suffering than anything I could ever dream of. I know now that the torture I have gone through was the consequence of my own actions, actions that were done through my own misunderstanding of everything—of life, of death, of me, of you, and of everything I had seen and have been through. Life will never be easy. It never was. Why should it change just because I wish it was so? Survival is earned.

There is a mystery to life and to death. We as mortal beings will never truly know what lies ahead. I try to find comfort in this mystery. Within this nothingness of the unknown lies potential. This place of strengths and weaknesses is a vast ocean of limitless potential. It's up to us to choose what happens next. Who cares who's watching? It's up to us to choose what happens next.

Life is about finding out who you really are beyond who you think you are, beyond who you've been taught you are, beyond your self-created story about who you are, beyond all images of who you are. Our inner conflict becomes our outer conflict. When I am at war within myself, I go to war with you. What I reject in myself, I reject in the world. That rejection leads to suffering of every kind. We avoid what we don't like about ourselves. We battle with painful emotions. We search for people, things, and situations that we hope will complete us. We desperately seek to escape our reality. The dualistic split in the present experience, in the separation of "me" from life itself, is where all human suffering, conflict, and violence originate. We must face our own present experience and heal the madness and separation there. Begin to clearly see and understand the suffering we create for ourselves, for others, and for our planet. Recognizing this truth leads us to total responsibility in the best sense of the word.

My future is waiting for me, so I will stop living in the past. I do not miss the shadows. When they would start to appear and move, I couldn't stop staring at them. I would swear they were real, but I was the only one that could see them. Is this for real? Do ghosts really exist in the shadows? Maybe they're all around us and we are all unaware of their presence.

While I was using and deep in my addictions, any feeling of discomfort would bring about the thought that this discomfort must not be tolerated. This discomfort must never happen ever again and must be stopped now. And the longer the uncomfortable feelings were there, the crazier I would feel. And the crazier I feel, the more I feel like I'm going to die or not make it through the day. Then I become overwhelmed with despair, anxiety, and panic. Then the panic grows. Fiending thoughts become as loud as screams in my head. There is no escaping at this point, or so I believed. And the only way to get out of it was to give my mind, body, and disease what it wanted.

Then the next day started over, and I could either let the panic creep in or use the drugs early to stop it before it starts. The drugs start off as a want. Then they become a need. This is a very dark and scary place to be when you realize the drugs have become a necessity to feeling normal.

Somewhere along the way, we become separated and disconnected. We feel misery, depression, anguish, and anxiety. I often hear people say "I just want to be happy." But this "want" is deeper than the desire to be happy. It's a desire and a search to be in a state a bliss. We desire what we once had, which is feeling like we belong, feeling like we matter, feeling connected with existence.

Reject nothing. To put it another way, accept everything. The big fear in the back of everyone's mind is death. Or rather, what happens to us after we die. It is true that one day our bodies will die. There's no way around that. But I believe that a positive perspective on death enables us to have a positive perspective on life. Do not fear death. Accept it as a truth, as part of the life cycle of all living things. Death is not the end all. I believe that death is a start to a new beginning. Rigid ideals create problems for us. The new ideal of death should be loosely defined because no one knows for sure what happens after death. But the theory does not have to be a gloomy one. And it does not have to be one theory.

One theory on death is that nothing happens. It's a permanent sensation of consciousness. Another theory on death is that your energy is transferred into another form. This theory can be argued by the scientific fact that energy is never destroyed, only transferred. This theory can be envisioned as the caterpillar into a butterfly metaphor. Or this simile: we are like a bubble of air. What happens to the bubble when it pops? The visible shape of the bubble is gone but not the material that was inside the bubble. The inner material (the soul) has returned to the infinite space that is our universe. The air we breathe is not empty at all.

The five stages of death are grief, denial, anger, depression, bargaining, and acceptance. I find it no surprise that the final stage is acceptance. Unconditionally accepting yourself naturally brings about your individual transformation. This is at the heart of everyone's situation because the greatest desire in the world is for inner transformation.

How do you define something that has no form? How do you define something that has no definite shape? The human soul is mysterious and beyond our human comprehension. We can compare it to what it's like. We can compare it to what it is not. But what we do know is that our parents and grandparents live on through us through our memory of them, through our actions and our personalities. They taught us how to live and how to love. We are a piece of them. We will carry on their legacy. We will pick up where they left off.

They live through us without us even realizing that they are. We are already a piece of them. We are already a reflection of them. Each one of them taught us how to live in their own unique way. They taught us how to walk, how to talk, how to eat, how to communicate. The rest is really up to us. Even though they are not here physically, spiritually they are living on through us. A piece of their personality is expressed through us, unconsciously.

Do you think about every word you're about to say before you say it? No. We just know how to communicate. We just know how to express what's going on inside us and how we're feeling. Do you think about every move you make in the shower? No. We just know what to do. Do you think about every turn you make while driving home from work? No. We know how to get there. Start to notice how much thoughtless action you take during your normal day. And by thoughtless action I don't mean careless action. I mean listening to your instincts and trusting them. Within your instincts is an ancient intelligence passed down to us by our ancestors.

This same thoughtless action applies for the painter. He is not thinking about every brushstroke or every color he uses. He's just letting it out. It's a thoughtless action of expression. The same applies to the singer. She is not thinking about every note she hits. She's just letting it out. She just knows what note to hit through her thoughtless action of expression. It's difficult to teach rhythm to someone. You can try to explain how to dance. You can give examples and demonstrations. But dance is another form of expression and communication. Some people just know how to do it without thinking. The movement of the body and the music become one. It's easy to tell if someone is thinking while they're dancing as opposed to someone who is dancing with no thought, only feeling. Dancing with feeling is way more genuine, and it clearly shows.

Now apply this moving with feeling to your everyday life. As you move through the day, listen to your instincts and trust them. Go with the flow of your instincts. In other words, listen to your heart more than your mind. You will be living more genuinely. You and existence become one. Past, present, and future become one in the present moment. Everything in your life up to now has been leading to this very moment. That will always be true. Make your choices and decisions by going with the flow. Of course, plan for the future, but don't stay there. Focus on where your feet are right now and be there.

Am I just a leaf being thrown around by the wind of the universe? From time to time I experience déjà vu—not every day and not every week but enough for it to get my attention. Is my life already written? Am I just a leaf being thrown around by the wind of the universe? God, please help us find our way.

I found this note I wrote to myself on November 6, 2020: "I lost my soul, and now I want it back. I'm trying to find my soul, and I don't know where to look." I have been running from the fear of uncertainty and the fear of failure for many years. But the only time I fail is when I run away. The reality is that there is nowhere to hide. I have to live my life the way it was meant to be lived: beautifully and artistically. I can no longer go backward. Life still goes on without my involvement, but it is infinitely better when I participate, when I assist, when I share my light with the dark uncertainty of the future.

Simulation Theory

The simulation theory doesn't work for me. If it makes sense to you, that's fine. But I can't accept it and live my life with that belief. I believe the world and universe we live in is real. When we call things illusions, it's referring to our self-projected perspective on our environment and our imagination. For example, as human beings, we are obsessed and consumed with the illusion of ourselves. We are indeed real. But we tend to forget about everything around us and are only concerned with our own personal welfare, our own individual personality, and satisfying our ego.

Sometimes our only concern is with what we want and what we don't have. I am definitely guilty of this myself, for sure. I tend to exaggerate the awfulness of my life or current circumstance and current responsibilities. I forget how good I have it. I forget that I used to be homeless. I forget that I'm a recovered alcoholic and addict. I forget that my childhood was pretty good. I forget that I came from a loving home. I forget that my parents are still together. I take for granted all the positive factors in my life because I'm always comparing my life to someone else who, I feel, has a better life than me. I forget to appreciate what I have.

That aside, this simulation theory is based on a probability. And since anything is possible, the simulation theory is probable. In my opinion, there is a very, very low chance. Maybe about the same chance I have at winning the lottery, and I don't even play. Anyway, the theory basically says that we are all living in a simulation—like a video game controlled by a "player."

I can understand how some people can feel like this makes sense. As you walk down the street, we walk by other people that we do not interact with. These would be the noninteracting characters in the simulation or game. If you watch these noninteracting characters, they can seem almost robotic. And the people you do interact with have only a small set of possible types of conversations. Like at work, for instance. If you watch closely, your conversations are somewhat repetitive with your coworkers and bosses. It can seem as if these conversations are "programmed" as an autopilot reaction and response.

But we are habitual creatures by nature. We have schedules, and these schedules are often very repetitive. Just like the planets and the moon have cycles around the sun, we wake up and pretty much do the same thing every day. We are cyclical just like the world around us. The sun rises, and so do we. The sun sets, and we go to bed. Again and again. Repetition can drive some people crazy, myself included. I really try to switch it up to break up the monotony of the everyday maintenance. So I understand how our lives can seem programmed.

Our computer code is our DNA. Under a microscope, we are made up of millions upon millions of cells and atoms. Under a strong enough microscope, one can argue that we are made of more space than physical matter. If we stand back far enough and look at planet

Earth from the moon, human beings are like a grain of sand in the desert, a drop of water in the ocean.

Some people may see this reality and think, *Why does my life matter? If I am just a grain of sand in the desert or a drop of water in the sea, why should I care about what I do?* My answer to that is: everything matters, and everything is important, from the big to the small, from the macroscopic to the microscopic. Everything is connected to everything. Each grain of sand plays a part. Each drop of water makes up the ocean. Obviously, there is more life in the ocean than in the desert. But the grain of sand and the drop of water are used only to illustrate the metaphor. Every drop of water is needed to make up the vast ocean that it is. Every drop of water in the ocean counts because it makes up the home for all ocean life.

I have come to believe that human beings evolved from the ocean. We evolved from single-celled organisms living in the ocean millions of years ago. If all those drops of water were not in the ocean, we would not be here today. From where you are sitting right now, everything matters, in all directions. From infinity in the negative direction to infinity in the positive direction, everything is connected. Everything affects everything. In short, everything you do now affects your future and the future of many people around you.

Time moves slowly, and you live with yourself all day, every day. At the very least, don't you want a peaceful life? Why wouldn't you want to do things that help create a quiet mind? It's not fun to feel like you're losing your mind and going crazy. I know it's not fun. I've been there. You might be looking for answers to complicated questions. I assure you, life is worth living. Truly living and experiencing life is enjoyable. It really can be, but you must make it so. Life doesn't just give you joy. You have to create it in your own unique way.

We have all been given the gift of free will. We can do whatever we want. Some people, including myself, have unconsciously chosen to live a miserable life. It's never too late to pull yourself out of the hole you have dug for yourself. I believe this to be true because if I can do it, then I believe anyone can. I'm lucky to be alive right now, and I never let myself forget that.

Is it possible that our solar system is just a cluster of cells in a giant's eyeball? Maybe. I don't know for sure. We do not have the technology to travel past enough galaxies to find out what is beyond what we can see. I use the eyeball metaphor because it is true that there are as many cells in your eye as there are stars in our galaxy. Amazing, right? There is an entire galaxy in each one of your eyes. Realizing this, we start to look at worlds within worlds within worlds.

The most popular theory we have is the big bang theory as the leading hypothesis as to how our universe was created. It sounds right to me. There could have been a big explosion that flung the elements as we know them into space. Those particles became clouds and clusters. Then those clouds became more and more dense, forming chemical reactions and fireballs. Then those fireballs collided into each other until stars and planets were formed. Or something along those lines. But what I'm interested in is, what caused the big bang? There had to be an intense buildup of pressure over a very long period of time. Because that's how explosions work.

Either way, something cannot be formed from nothing. Even the empty space in outer space is not empty. Star dust, molecules, and atoms are floating through that empty space. We just can't see it without a microscope. In short, the big bang theory states that the universe began with every speck of its energy jammed into a very tiny point. This extremely dense point exploded with unimaginable force, creating matter and propelling it outward to make the billions of galaxies of our vast universe.

So every spec of the universe's energy was jammed into a very tiny point? What was forcing this "jamming" effect? We could say God. We can definitely say a power greater than ourselves. But simulation theorists will say the creator of the game, the creator of the simulation we live in, created the universe. And how do we please the creator? We do our best to improve upon the simulation itself. This is pretty much the same thing religions will tell you about how our past ancestors did their best to please their gods. They tried to improve upon the world that they had been given, which shows appreciation for their life. Isn't it true that we should appreciate the fact that we are alive? Are you comfortable believing or accepting that a "player" is controlling you as you journey through this "simulation" we call life?

This is a conversation that could go on forever. It's an interesting topic. It can be considered. But for me, my gods are not in the shape of a human being. I have come to believe that there are forces at work that created and maintain the universe. Those forces are what I call God. It is an intelligence far greater than I can comprehend as a human being. I am fascinated by the forces of the universe, loyal to them, and I trust God completely. Trusting the forces that created and maintain the universe has proven to be the sanest way for me to live.

Contentment Versus Enlightenment

I believe striving for contentment is great place to start on the spiritual journey to quieting the mind. From a place of contentment, enlightenment can be found. I am starting to believe that enlightenment is not just one single place you reach as a destination. I believe that the term *enlightenment* is casually thrown around as a place only reached by lifelong practices of meditation.

I have come to believe that enlightenment has degrees, similar to a light bulb's color, temperature, and brightness. The brighter the bulb, the higher number of lumens. So the more enlightened you become, the more you can "see." Or the more aware you become, the more enlightened you become. Enlightenment is not achieved on your first attempt. Neither is contentment. But in my experience, contentment is much easier to reach.

My definition of contentment is being satisfied and pleased with your environment and inner well-being. A peaceful mind exists when what you believe to be true matches what you see in your environment. It is the disappearance of wanting. It is being able to step way back to see the big picture. It is seeing the past, present, and future all at once and being pleased with it. Through this peaceful perspective, enlightenment begins to unfold and grows brighter. When speaking in terms of spirituality, there is no ceiling and there is no floor, no good or bad. There are no limitations. There are no defined numbers. There are no boundaries. Only the direction of infinity in the positive and negative direction.

Here is something important to consider: you must give yourself permission to be content because there are a few things standing in our way to being content. One of them is the ego, which is the inner child that kicks and screams until it gets what it wants. Then it kicks and screams for something else. And that can go on for a lifetime if you let your ego call the shots.

The goal here is to realize that accumulating more things does not create contentment. The seeking for contentment through things is a losing battle. You must be able to let go of your things. The material things are yours but will never be you. And if you are not careful, those material things end up owning you, not the other way around. It's nice to have nice things, but don't define yourself by what you have accumulated. That kind of perspective is working in the opposite direction of contentment.

A better way to define yourself is by way of your character. It really doesn't matter what you look like or what you have. What is important are your principles and values. What your morals and standards are. This is what we all need to focus on, myself included. I am far from perfect. I have weakness, insecurities, and take things for granted that I shouldn't. But we must be able to recognize our weaknesses. And by recognizing them when they appear, we can begin to turn them into strengths by using self-control, restraint, and wisdom from learned experiences.

I believe we all want peace and comfort. From comfort and peace comes happiness and love. Fundamentally, these are spiritual goals. The difficult part is to take our personal selves out of our own personal existence. In other words, do not only think and only have concern for yourself. The world is very big, and there are millions of life-forms on this planet. You are not the only one with wants, needs, and problems. For every action there is an equal but opposite reaction. In other words, you get what you give.

When we focus on where we would rather be, we immediately reject the present moment. This is the beginning of suffering. To live artistically is to create a new and unique level of attention and energy to each moment that the moment deserves. The majority of our thoughts are coming from the limited data that we have gathered during our lifetime.

Some thoughts we can create using our will, and some thoughts can be aligned with the universe and the intelligence that holds up the planets. When we start dissolving our individual personality and align ourselves with this universal intelligence, we begin to realize and see ourselves as the same as all life. This is where separation ends and unity begins. Unity is the realization of the one energy that is within everything living and nonliving. This energy force is what I believe to be God.

We do not need war to obtain peace. Life is peaceful naturally. Yes, there is turbulence from time to time. And animals hunt and eat other animals. But the peace is maintained. We as humans complicate life by creating problems and cause separation.

I have come to believe that our purpose is to transcend our limited thinking and awaken our ultimate potential, our infinite potential. We need to constantly practice increasing our level of awareness. There is no top line and no bottom line. It is up to us to choose our life, our living situation, and our inner well-being. The inner workings of our psychology can be mysterious. It is unfamiliar territory. It has been my life's work to figure this out and improve on it because I have been living with confusion as long as I can remember. I was scared, fearful, confused, and did not really know what I was doing. Only since recently could I see more clearly. Everything that I have learned during my life is starting to make sense, which is allowing me to continue going forward with my understanding of this life that I am living in.

We all have a lesson to be learned. Each person has their own tailored lesson or teaching to be realized. Once we have fully understood what we are to learn, we should be practicing these teachings. We should accept these lessons on the deepest of levels and truly believe it as the right thing to believe as the truth. Through our practice of our newfound realizations, we begin to teach all we encounter.

We are not choosing to teach, but we become teachers and guides on a meaningful, spiritual, and deep level.

You can't always see it, but you can feel it. You can experience and feel it deep within your being—a connection, a oneness with everything in the universe. Past, present, and future are all happening in this moment. You disappear and become everything, or everything disappears and you become nothing. In an instant, you are no longer a separate individual struggling to find wholeness. There is only wholeness, and you continue to function in the world effortlessly.

How to find awareness? How to identify with the real you? How to experience a connection and unity with the universe? How to identify with all life-forms? What is our true identity? Start from within then move your focus outward. Use your imagination to see yourself floating up into space and looking down upon the earth. Then bring yourself down back to earth but shrinking to the size of a grain of sand. Then move back slowly up to your human form. Focus on your awareness. Focus on your ability to focus.

What are you aware of? Who is the one who receives the thoughts? Who is the one who observes the thoughts? Begin to realize how vast your awareness is. It is infinite. Feel the activity within your body. Witness your heartbeat without holding your hand there. Feel your pulse. Feel the subtle electric current that is constantly flowing through you. Feel your blood moving throughout your entire body. Realize that you don't have to tell your heart to beat. It works on its own. Your eyes blink on their own. If you get an itch, your hand scratches it on its own. Your mind produces thoughts on its own just as the heart beats on its own.

Your awareness, your soul, is the witness to all this bodily activity. The real you is your soul, your spirit. Your spirit has no form and no defined boundary just as the emptiness of space has no form. But the space of the universe is not empty. It contains all contents of the universe, allowing them to exist. Your spirit is the vast awareness that contains your body and mind and allows all thought and emotion to exist. This is what to identify with. Do not identify with what you look like. Not with what your intellect is telling you how you should be. Not the illusion your ego has formed about yourself. Identify with your infinite awareness, with your divine spirit. This is the real you. Your body has been changing and evolving since your conception. Your soul has remained unchanged and untouched. Identify with your awareness. Identify with your spirit.

Hold your hand in front of your face and relax your eyes. Allow yourself to have double vision in that your one hand becomes two. As you keep your double vision on your hand, become aware of what is past your hand. Keep your eyes relaxed, keep your head still, then become aware of what is to your left. Become aware of what is to your right. Where is the exit door? Envision what is past the door. You just traveled outside your room without leaving your seat because your awareness traveled outside while your body remained inside. I know this sounds like nonsense, but let's analyze this for a minute.

There is no limit to how far your awareness can reach. By placing your awareness on a friend and remembering fun adventures you've shared, in turn, your friend will start to remember those same feelings about you. Have you ever called someone and they said, "I was just about to call you." Or they say, "I was just thinking about you." We all share this mysterious and interesting telekinesis with each other.

It is true that we use about 10 percent of our brain during our normal every day. But what can the remaining 90 percent do? As humans, there are things that we have difficulty comprehending. And spirituality is one of them. My ability to fully understand and explain spirituality is limited. All I can say is what I have experienced and what I have come to believe. And I have come to believe because it truly makes sense to me. It feels right. I have learned that when it feels right in my heart, then it's worth me believing that it is true.

The first step when seeking spiritual wisdom is to become willing to accept that you are not your body nor your mind. To become willing is the first step; the belief comes later. You must be willing to accept that the real you is not your thoughts nor your emotion. From that acceptance you realize that the real you is your soul, your spirit, your awareness, your consciousness. These are all the same things.

How do you define something that has no shape or form to define it? That which has no form is infinite.

Our awareness is like water in that it takes the shape of anything it's placed in or placed upon. Your awareness is the observer, the silent witness to all you experience. I envision my spirit as a silhouette of my body that exists behind my skin but is not bound to the defined shape of my body. Your spirit observes everything you experience without judgment. It is your ego and intellect that make the determinations, judges, and decides what is favorable and what is unfavorable. Your spirit exists wherever you place your attention and focus.

Sometimes we lose focus because we start paying more attention to the thoughts that are appearing in our mind rather than paying attention to the person who is speaking or the book that we are reading. You are wherever your attention is. Do not give much significance to your thoughts. Create a space between you and your thoughts. Observe your thoughts from a distance and do not label them or judge them. Allow them to appear then disappear.

As one disappears, another thought will appear. But there is a space in between your thoughts. In between thoughts there is silence. In between thoughts is infinite wisdom. Become the observer of your thoughts. Do not allow yourself to become your thoughts. I understand that this is easier said than done. It took me a while just to grasp this concept. But this is not a concept, it is a practice. This is what you will hear gurus and spiritual advisors say a lot. It is important to only observe, without judgment.

How quick are we to label and judge just about everything we see? The spiritual practice is to observe only. Do not engage your thoughts, do not entertain them, do not label them. Just observe. Become the witness of everything going on within you. Isn't it amazing that your body operates completely on its own? Now with that same focus of being the observer of within, focus your attention outward. Observe what you see, but do not label it. Observe the shapes, observe the light, observe the shadow, and observe the space in between objects. Recognize and relate to the space between objects. This is important to get familiar with because the space between objects represents and is related to the space between you and your thoughts and emotions. The space is where the real you exists.

What sounds are appearing within you? Can you hear cars? Do you hear birds? Can you hear the wind? Is there a subtle ring in your ears? You can only experience the world from within yourself. The entire world, the entire universe, exists within you. Our senses are outward bound, but we experience everything from within. Become an observer of this world, and all you will see is beauty and wonder.

While sitting still, I listen to and feel my heartbeat. I begin to feel my pulse in my arms and in my legs. I can feel my skin tingle. I can almost control giving myself the chills up the back of my neck then throughout my entire body. I take a quick breath in and hold it for a few seconds then release it slowly. With each quick breath in, I focus on the back of my neck where my head meets my spine. I continue my quick breath in then slow release, and on the release, I receive a wave of what I can best describe as the chills, sent from the back of my neck through my arms and legs. This is how I meditate. It only takes a few minutes a day to find unity within myself and my universe.

CHAPTER 30

A MESSAGE TO MY UNBORN SON OR DAUGHTER

You were made from me and your mother's love, just as I was made from my parents' love. Just as your mother was made from her parents' love. I have come to believe that all living things were made from the love of God. But that's another conversation that you and I will have when you learn to speak.

Right now, your mother is reading this and absorbing this information, and through her amazing circulatory system, so are you. I wanted to let you know how incredible you are. How important you are. How much you are loved and cherished. I wanted to let you know that I have been thinking about you long before you were conceived. You were planned. Your mother and I have become well prepared to bring you into this world. This is a beautiful place to live. You will make it beautiful through your perspective. This world becomes exactly how you see it. If you see it as a dark and cold place, that's what it will be. If you see it as a wondrous and amazing creation, that's what it will be.

You can do anything you want. You can be anything you want to become. But you must dedicate yourself and work hard for it. We can only show you the way how and point you in the right direction. It will be up to you to take the first step into your own individuality.

Your choices affect your environment and situations. And your situations and environment are a direct result of your choices. You will not be able to control everything, but there is a great deal of what you can control. You must learn the difference. You must learn what you can do and what you cannot do. I know this is a lot of information that may be confusing, or you may begin forming doubts. But we can simplify this for you.

See and treat everyone the same: with loving acceptance, just as you would have them see and treat you. If you give respect, you receive respect. Never allow yourself to forget that your life is a gift from God. You are very lucky to be alive and healthy. That will become more obvious as you travel through life.

Acceptance is the key to freedom. Allow everything to pass through your five senses. The more you resist and reject life, the more painful your life will become. God will never give you more than what you can handle. The most important place for you to be is where you are right now. This will always be true throughout your entire life. But start with right now. Right now, you are growing, getting stronger and evolving. The process you are going through right now is not in your control. Please understand this to be true. Allow the natural process of your birth to take place. This is a slow process, so be patient. Have faith and put your trust in creation, in this ancient intelligence. Don't try too hard to comprehend it. Just allow life to unfold for you.

We will teach you how to focus your attention for long periods of time. Strengthening your ability to focus is the key to your success. Your focus and attention, your awareness and consciousness, your soul and spirit are all the same things. This is the real you. Your awareness is your superpower, and it will always be with you. Your body and mind will change and evolve, but your spirit will always remain the same, infinite. We will teach you how to recognize it and how to find unity. Your potential is limitless. Your ability to include everything and everyone is infinite. You now have a life of your own, but you share life with all living things. Experience everything in the world as yourself.

You can come to me and your mother at any time and ask for help with whatever you need assistance with. We will always be here for you. We are letting you know now that life is not easy. It's not supposed to be. You will learn that anything worth having is not easy to obtain. It is also not impossible. If you dedicate yourself and work for it and keep your attention on what you desire, it will eventually become part of your life. Your dreams can become your reality.

I have been given another second chance, and I thank God for it every day. I will raise you to be a prince and, eventually, the king of your world. All the while a servant to God and your universe. I will show you how to find your inner strength. You will discover that you have the ability to mold your future. I will teach you how to find your voice. I am doing everything in my power to become a great provider for you and the family. No one is demanding this, but I have made a promise to myself and to God to take on this responsibility.

Rest well, little one. You have a lot to look forward to. And so do we. Allow us to love you the best way we know how, and you will see that the most natural thing you can do is love us back.

Emotional Well-being

I have self-destructive weaknesses that makes me do very stupid things. I am compulsive. I am impatient. I want it all or nothing. And since I don't have it all right now, I throw it all away and don't save anything for the future. Therefore, I have struggled my entire life to get ahead.

I'm a little upset it has taken me thirty-seven years to get it right. I try to find comfort and pride in the fact that it didn't take me thirty-eight years. Now my fight is not over turf or personality. I am fighting over how to best serve my world. It's a silly but noble fight. We are all good men and women just trying to do what's right. I am a follower and a leader. I am paying close attention to my environment to tell me which one to be at this moment. I am not looking to take anyone's job. The only way for me to receive is to have it willingly handed to me.

The bottom line is that nothing is worth throwing away all your hard work, all the progress you have made, and in turn, your very possible bright future. Stay distracted from evil. Work out. Meet other alcoholics and keep in constant communication. Read AA-sponsored books, self-help books, and spiritually guiding books. Find a sponsor, which is someone you get along with and relate to on an emotional level. Your sponsor is responsible for taking you through the Twelve Steps. You and your sponsor will become lifelong friends.

Keep in touch with your family and repair broken relationships. Their trust in you will increase with time. Their trust then turns into belief in you. Find a job. You need your own money to pay your own bills and also to pay back any debt you may have. Go back to school. Work toward earning a degree in what you see yourself doing for the rest of your life. A college loan is not that difficult to get. Discover and cultivate a hobby. Create things your way. Proudly display them for yourself as a reminder that you are indeed a talented and well-rounded person. This is also a therapeutic way to express yourself in tangible ways.

Save your money. A little bit of saving goes a long way in time. This takes a lot of patience, but saving money naturally happens when you stop buying things you don't need. Attend as many holidays as possible, birthday parties, weddings, and baby showers. Make an effort to get to know your aunts, uncles, and cousins. The love of your family is important and must be shared. Go to the doctor to get your yearly physical. Go to the dentist to get your teeth cleaned. Eat healthy.

When you get thoughts and reminders of how you used to drink and get high, you will cringe in disgust. You will be able to say to yourself, "I can't believe I used to do that." Your new view on drugs will be that it is poison. No more lying to yourself in thinking that it will make you feel better. No more lying to yourself. Drugs only make you and everything around you worse. Drugs take everything away, and I mean *everything*.

Choose soda or juice over beer every time. You are probably only craving the sugar anyway. Learn to relax and sit still. Within stillness is wisdom. When you see other people drinking and getting high, see them as yourself. Recognize that this is how you used to be. Accept that it may work for them but know that it no longer works for you. When you see homeless people, see them as yourself. Recognize that this could be you if you would have continued on your destructive path.

Understand how lucky you are to be alive. Each new day is an amazing gift from what you perceive to be God. Thank God every morning for restoring you to sanity. Thank God for your health and pray for strength, wisdom, and the courage to make it through this day sober. Pray for the happiness of others, for your friends and your enemies. See the beauty in the world. Look forward to what today is about to bring you, the good and the bad. Because it's all good.

Become satisfied with what you do have. I guarantee you there is someone out there that wishes they had what you have. Don't envy the life of another person. I guarantee you that if you were to live their life, you would miss yours and want it back. Make your choices wisely. Each choice you have ever made has led you to this moment right now. Live each day with your head held straight and your shoulders back. Your posture and how you hold yourself is crucial to your inner well-being.

Believe in yourself. Listen to your heart, and be honest with yourself. Whatever you honestly feel is the right thing to do, I'm sure it will be the right thing. Live with grace in this chaotic, beautiful world. Be rough and delicate at the same time. Your soul has never left you. It has always been there and always will be. You have found yourself.

Some days are harder than others. You are going to have to power through it, my friend. But don't do it alone. You know what happens when we're left alone for too long. When you're having a difficult time and you feel like you're starting to go crazy, pick up the phone and call someone. Anyone. Talk about it, and let it out. Preferably someone you can relate to on an emotional level. This is the most important thing for an addict to learn how to do because this will keep you sane. This is how AA was started—by two alcoholics talking to each other.

We relate to each other by understanding exactly what the other is saying and understanding exactly how they feel. It sounds too simple to be true, but that's the majority of the work to restoring your sanity and lifting your obsession. The point is, you cannot do this on your own; so there is no shame in asking for help or asking to talk to someone. We all must do it. Not only is it emotionally healthy but it is also part of being human.

Your emotional well-being is the most valuable to your sobriety, and it is very difficult to achieve this on your own. We must learn to become comfortable with talking about the uncomfortable—talking about your past, talking about your pain, and talking about your problems. After that you can talk about your plans, about your wishes and desires, and figuring out what action is needed to reach those goals. Your emotions can only hurt you if you hold them in. Just by talking about it cuts your pain in half.

We are all artists. The painter must paint. The sculptor must sculpt. The writer must write. The singer must sing. Our individual experience of life is built by how we perceive and by what we create. What kind of a world will you paint? The paintbrush is always in your hand.

UPON AWAKENING

Please allow me to leave you with one last inspirational thought, a passage from the *Big Book of Alcoholics Anonymous*, pages 86–88:

> On awakening let us think about the twenty-four hours ahead. We consider our plans for the day. Before we begin, we ask God to direct our thinking, especially asking that it be divorced from self-pity, dishonest or self-seeking motives. Under these conditions we can employ our mental faculties with assurance, for after all God gave us brains to use. Our thought of life will be placed on a much higher plane when our thinking is cleared of wrong motives.
>
> In thinking about our day, we may face indecision. We may not be able to determine which course to take. Here we ask God for inspiration, an intuitive thought, or a decision. We relax and take it easy. We don't struggle. We are often surprised how the right answers come after we have tried this for a while.
>
> What used to be the hunch, or the occasional inspiration gradually becomes a working part of the mind. Being still inexperienced and having just made conscious contact with God, it is not probable that we are going to be inspired at all times. We might pay for this presumption in all sorts of absurd actions and ideas. Nevertheless,

we find that our thinking will, as time passes, be more and more on the plane of inspiration. We come to rely upon it.

We usually conclude the period of meditation with a prayer that we be shown all through the day what our next step is to be, that we be given whatever we need to take care of such problems. We ask especially for freedom from self-will and are careful to make no request for ourselves only. We may ask for ourselves, however, if others will be helped. We are careful never to pray for our own selfish ends. Many of us have wasted a lot of time doing that and it doesn't work. You can easily see why.

If circumstances warrant, we ask our wives or friends to join us in morning meditation. If we belong to a religious denomination which requires a definite morning devotion, we attend to that also. If not members of religious bodies, we sometimes select and memorize a few set prayers which emphasize the principles we have been discussing. There are many helpful books also. Suggestions about these may be obtained from one's priest, minister, or rabbi. Be quick to see where religious people are right. Make use of what they offer.

As we go through the day we pause, when agitated or doubtful, and ask for the right thought or action. We constantly remind ourselves we are no longer running the show, humbly saying to ourselves many times each day "Thy will be done." We are then in much less danger of excitement, fear, anger, worry, self-pity, or foolish decisions. We become much more efficient. We do not tire so easily, for we are not burning up energy foolishly as we did when we were trying to arrange life to suit ourselves.

It works—it really does.

OUTRO

This is a book about life—my life, your life, and all life, from the smallest life-forms to the largest. This is a book about the past, the present, and the possible future. I believe all people have unique qualities that make them individuals. I also believe, on a fundamental level, that all people are the same. If I can understand my life, I can understand all life.

We absorb and harness the power of the sun. We absorb and harness the energy that trees emit. We all breathe the same air and stand on the same ground. We are connected to everything in our universe, and everything in our universe is connected to us. Science has taught us that energy can never be destroyed, only transferred. By inference, my life does not vanish at the moment of my death. My life is transferred back into the universe, back from where it came. Life and death are mysterious. I believe that there is no right or wrong answer when discussing the possibilities of what happens when we die. Therefore, I believe that there is no right or wrong religion. I appreciate the teachings of all religions.

I have described the facts and have recalled the events that have taken place in my life for the sole purpose of learning from my past, so I am better prepared for the future. I have dissected my strengths and weaknesses. I will not let my weaknesses define me as a person. By acknowledging my weaknesses and not allowing them to control my actions, I turn my weaknesses into strengths.

I want to empower and inspire you. Wisdom should be available to anyone who seeks it. I am by no means a sage, oracle, or guru. I am just a man who has experienced tragedies, suffered through terrible addictions, and have made it through to tell my story with the intention of helping the next suffering individual. I want you to find relief from your emotional suffering. I want you to gain the ability to quiet your mind. Emotional healing begins with relating to another human being on a deep emotional level.

My intent is to help. To anyone who is looking for answers, this is open to interpretation. This is for you. Thank you for your support, time, and attention.

Bibliography

Chopra, Deepak. *Life After Death: The Burden of Proof.* New York: Three Rivers Press, 2006.

Ellis, Albert, J. F. McInerney, R. DiGiuseppe, and R. J. Yeager. *Relational-Emotive Therapy with Alcoholics and Substance Abusers.* Massachusetts: Allyn and Bacon, 1988.

Foster, Jeff. *The Deepest Acceptance: Radical Awakening in Ordinary Life.* Colorado: Sounds True, Inc., 2012.

Osho. *Emotional Wellness: Transforming Fear, Anger, and Jealousy into Creative Energy.* United States: Harmony Books, 2007.

Peck, M. Scott, MD. *The Road Less Traveled.* New York: Touchstone, 1978.

Ramanasramam, Sri. *The Spiritual Teaching of Ramana Maharshi.* Colorado: Shambhala Publications, Inc., 1972.

Sadhguru. *Inner Engineering: A Yogi's Guide to Joy.* New York: Spiegel & Grau, 2016.

Singer, Michael A. *The Untethered Soul.* California: New Harbinger Publications Inc., 2007.

Tolle, Eckhart. *The Power of Now: A Guide to Spiritual Enlightenment.* Canada: Namaste Publishing, 1999.

Tyson, Neil deGrasse. *Astrophysics for People in a Hurry.* New York: W. W. Norton & Company Inc., 2017.

W. Bill and Dr. Bob. *Alcoholics Anonymous.* 4th ed. New York City: A.A. World Services Inc., 2001.

Zukav, Gary. *The Seat of the Soul.* New York: Simon & Schuster Paperbacks, 1989.

ABOUT THE AUTHOR

Christopher Rizzo was born 11/11/1983 and lives in Manhattan. From the age of sixteen, he has been working in the field of construction. Christopher struggled to get through the politics of high school then also fought an uphill battle to get through college and, at this point, had already gone through a lifetime's worth of heartbreak, trauma, depression, and insanity.

With a shattered heart and a knot in his stomach, he became emotionally sick. Wonderment of the world and hopes for a bright future disappeared. Christopher gave up on his own self-respect and became obsessed with his own self-destruction. He earned a bachelor's degree in engineering and landed a good job in the city but was an empty shell of a human.

Christopher has been through inpatient rehabs, overdoses, homelessness, and jails all because of his insidious drug addiction to heroin. After about twelve years of living in hell, he became determined to search for heaven. At this point in his life, he had been to AA meetings, but his attendance was always mandated by either the state of New York or by family. Christopher now made a conscious choice to seek help on his own. He had read Step 1 before but never really understood what it was asking, which is the full and complete acceptance that he is an addict and that if he wanted to live to see the next day, he could no longer get high. Not even a little bit. Because that was the thought that always took him back out.

Once Christopher truly accepted that he could no longer use drugs and let go of all reservations and resentments, his attitude toward life and himself began to change. He saw heroin as poison instead of medicine. He was no longer fighting against the current of life; he was swimming alongside it. With the help of medical professionals and his involvement in the program of AA, Christopher recently celebrated one year of consistent sobriety for the first time in his life. He has attended many public-speaking events by spiritual gurus and has read countless books on addiction, spirituality, religion, science, and psychology. He attends weekly AA meetings all over the city and is invited as the speaker every few months.

Christopher married the woman who stood by his side through the worst of times, and now they are experiencing the best of times. Their son was born on November 20, 2021. Christopher feels as though he has lived several lifetimes. He has found meaning and purpose in his life again and is now doing everything he can to reach out to other suffering individuals.

This book takes you through his struggle to get back onto his feet and every lesson he has learned along the way for the sole purpose of the reader to learn from his mistakes. And if you have made similar mistakes, he provides a path to repair them. Christopher believes this book has a lot of potential to help, motivate, and reach many people on an emotional level.

www.ingramcontent.com/pod-product-compliance
Lightning Source LLC
Chambersburg PA
CBHW061406280526
45784CB00001B/381